P9-BIO-226

WATCH-WORD!!!

A Glossary of Gobbledygook, Clichés, and Solecisms.

by
Argus John Tresidder

formerly Professor of English
Marine Corps Command and Staff College

Published by the
Marine Corps Association
Quantico, Virginia
1981

Copyright© 1981 Marine Corps Association

Library of Congress
Catalogue Card No. 81-82078
ISBN: O-940-328-00-3

All rights reserved. No part of this book may
be reproduced in any form without the permission of the Marine Corps Association.

TABLE OF CONTENTS

I have used the following dictionaries in my admittedly biased research:

1. *The American Heritage Dictionary of the English Language,* American Heritage Publishing Co. and Houghton Mifflin Co., New York, 1967.

2. *Clarence L. Barnhart Dictionary of New English Since 1963,* New York, Harper and Row, 1973.

3. Bergen and Cornelia Evans, *A Dictionary of Contemporary American Usage,* New York, Random House, 1957.

4. *Department of Defense Dictionary of Military and Associated Terms,* Joint Chiefs of Staff Publication 1, U.S. Government Printing Office, 1974.

5. Homer, Joel *JARGON:How to Talk to Anyone About Anything,* Times Books, 1979.

*6. William and Mary Morris, *Harper Dictionary of Contemporary Usage,* Harper and Row, New York, 1975

7. *Heath's Standard French and English Dictionaries,* Heath, New York, 1965.

8. *The Oxford English Dictionary,* Clarendon Press, Oxford, 1933.

9. *The Random House Dictionary of the English Language,* Random House, New York, 1966.

10. *Webster's New International Dictionary,* 2nd Edition, G. and C. Merriam Company, Springfield, Massachusetts, 1951.

11. *Webster's Third New International Dictionary,* G. and C. Merriam Company, Springfield, Massachusetts, 1964.

12. *Webster's New World Dictionary of the American Language,* World Publishing Company, New York, 1966.

---

* The Harper Panel, quoted several times, was a group of 136 prominent writers, editors, public speakers, educators, and commentators, whose opinions on matters of controversial usage were sought and recorded in *The Harper Dictionary.*

INTRODUCTION

The words that I shall discuss are in common use among American speakers and writers, particularly but by no means exclusively by the military. Most are examples of the gobbledygook which infests all professional groups and which, like bedbugs, has extended its pungent presence to the general public. A few like *reclama, relateral tell,* and *camouflet* are purely military words, included because their meaning is limited or because they are linguistically interesting. I have tried to avoid the purely technical words which are indispensable in some professional communication, but which the considerate speaker or writer should use sparingly unless he is addressing those familiar with his mysteries. Inclusion in the GLOSSARY does not necessarily mean condemnation. Many of the words are acceptable in informal communication and some are correct, but often abused or misused.

My point of view in listing these words is, quite honestly, that of the stubborn but discouraged believer in old-fashioned principles of language development. I do not agree with those makers of dictionaries who believe that a bastardized word like *orientate* or *liaise* becomes standard just because a number of misguided people use it. The sanctioned blurring of originally clear distinctions between *imply* and *infer,* for example, the wanton castration of words like *disinterested,* the permissive mispronunciation of *cerebral, flaccid, nuclear, phraseology, diphtheria*—make me sick (or as the unobservant speaker would say, make me nauseous!).

Those who like free and easy innovation in language had better put aside this glossary, which could raise their blood pressure. They will, no doubt rightly, regard its author as a Canute, hopelessly trying to halt the tide of sloppy neologisms, nouns warped into verbs, illiteracies, and barbarisms that threatens to engulf us (and to pollute our dictionaries).

More tolerant readers may say, "There, there. Let's not get so excited about structural linguists or whatever they call the people who think that usage is the criterion of acceptability. The English language is strong and healthy and can easily survive the sickness of 'Like wow, man' and 'outasite' and 'humungus' and *data* and *media* as singular nouns. As a matter of fact, don't you find that some of the words you hate have been in use for centuries?"

Of course they are right, and I'm spinning my aging, smooth tires. My study of gobbledygook has revealed that much of it has been long accepted even by the older (and better) dictionaries than the Merriam Third. My probably indefensible position is that usage doesn't necessarily make words *good.*

With these caveats (or, as the language contaminators would say, "having caveated the reader"), I shall begin my highly subjective list. Please forgive me if I step on some of your favorite words or misrepresent professional usage. Don't get mad when you discover that you regularly offend against some of my arbitrary rulings. You have plenty of company. But you might try to get rid of the most outrageous examples of poor usage.

ABBREVIATIONS USED IN THE TEXT

American Heritage: *THE AMERICAN HERITAGE DICTIONARY OF THE ENGLISH LANGUAGE.*

Barnhart: *CLARENCE L. BARNHART DICTIONARY OF NEW ENGLISH.*

Cf.: from the Latin *confer* means "compare."

DOD: *Department of Defense DICTIONARY OF MILITARY AND ASSOCIATED TERMS.*

e.g.: for example.

Evans: Bergen and Cornelia Evans, *A DICTIONARY OF CONTEMPORARY AMERICAN USAGE.*

Harper: *HARPER DICTIONARY OF CONTEMPORARY USAGE.*

L.: Latin.

MW2: *WEBESTER'S NEW INTERNATIONAL DICTIONARY, 2nd Edition.*

MW3: *WEBSTER'S THIRD NEW INTERNATIONAL DICTIONARY.*

Newman: Edwin Newman, author of *Strictly Speaking* and *A Civil Tongue.*

New World: *WEBSTER'S NEW WORLD DICTIONARY OF THE AMERICAN LANGUAGE.*

OED: *The OXFORD ENGLISH DICTIONARY.*

q.v.: from the Latin *quod vide* means "which see."

Random House: *THE RANDOM HOUSE DICTIONARY OF THE ENGLISH LANGUAGE.*

ABORT   is a verb meaning to miscarry or come to nothing. "To *abort* a mission" makes sense, but to say that a "mission was an *abort*" is a messy use of the word, in spite of the Merriam Third. The Department of Defense *Dictionary* lists *abort* only as a noun meaning "failure to accomplish a mission for reason other than enemy action." The OED says that the use of *abort* as a noun is obsolete.

ABOVE,   meaning "previously mentioned," is probably useful to lawyers, who don't care about graceful language. It is usually unnecessary, since what is "above" is clearly evident. In a speech, of course, it is absurd, unless the message is divine. If you *must* use it, at least refrain from making it into a noun: "Look carefully at *the above.*"

ACCEPT, EXCEPT   are a slippery pair, but only a dunce confuses them. *Accept* is always a verb; *except* is also a verb meaning "to exclude," but more often a preposition.

ACCESS   is a noun, not a verb, in spite of the creators of computerese.

ACCESSORIZE   is one of the worst of the -ize words. Don't use it, ever. And if you must use it, don't pronounce it "assessorize."

ACCLIMATE   may be pronounced both uh-KLĪ-mit and *AK-lih-mate.*

ACCOMPLISH   is a perfectly good word made to do more work than necessary. It means "to do," "to succeed in doing," or "to complete." The trouble with *accomplish* is not that it is wrongly used, but, no doubt because it conveys a triumphant sense of achievement, it is often used where another word would be better. We tend to speak about "accomplishing a mission." Let's occasionally try "fulfilling," "carrying out," or "completing" a mission, "achieving a goal," "performing a task," or just "doing" instead of always "accomplishing."

ACQUISITION   is a noun. Don't let anybody turn it into verb in imitation of *requisition.*

ACRONYMS   are useful abbreviations of phrases, titles, names, etc. by use of the first letters (or first few letters) of the words. Some neologisms, e.g., *radar, snafu,* and *sonar,* are acronyms. Too many acronyms are used without explanation, to the bewilderment of the uninformed. If you must use them, put them in parentheses after spelling out the whole the first time (unless they are as familiar as NATO, GOP, UN, etc.)

ACTION   has come to mean more than something done or physical combat. To be "where the *action* is" suggests that elsewhere is Dullsville. "To get a piece of the action" has a sinister ring to it. These meanings are not yet acceptable in formal writing.

ACTUALIZE.   Forget such revolting bastardizations.

ADAPT, ADOPT   are a slippery pair. *Adapt* means "to adjust oneself to a new or changed situation; *adopt* means "to choose and follow a new course of action" or "to make a child legally a member of a family." You can't *adopt* yourself to some one's ideas.

ADDITIONALLY   is an adverb meaning "in addition." It is obsessively and pompously used instead of "moreover," too often modifying a verb with which it has no real business: "Additionally, the sergeant laughed at the suggestion." Let up on this one, and on its more preposterous colleague, "hopefully."

ADDRESS   should not be used, as it too often is, in the sense of "comment on" or "discuss," as "I shall now *address* the subject of a volunteer army." The correct use is: "I shall *address* myself to the subject, etc." You can *address* an audience, but not an idea or a topic or, worst of all, an area. See **speak to a topic.**

ADJUSTMENTED   is a hideous error for *adjusted,* part of our fashionable habit of turning nouns into verbs.

ADMITTANCE   is not the same as *admission,* though they are close, and many use them interchangebly. Keep *admittance* for physically entering, *admission* for entrance involving permission, as to a club or by virtue of payment to a theatre. You can say *"admission* of guilt" or *"admission* of evidence." *Admittance* would be wrong in these figurative uses of the word.

ADVERSARY RELATIONSHIP   is current military gobbledygook for "enemy," which is a simple, clearly understood noun, overshadowed by fancy words like *adversaries* and *hostiles.*

ADVERSE, AVERSE   are a slippery pair. *Adverse* means against, antagonistic, unfavorable; *averse* means feeling distaste or repugnance.

ADVISE   in the sense of "inform" is the usage of old-fashioned, dull business-letter writers. "This is to advise you that your order of the 16th instant has been received and appreciated" is stuffy writing.

8

ADVISEE, ESCAPEE, ETC.   We seem to enjoy putting suffixes like -ee and -wise on words to turn them into squashy nouns. *Employee* (or *employe,* or *employé*) is a respectable French past participle which has become an English noun, in contrast to *employer.* We just can't arbitrarily assume, however, that -ee transforms all doers into receivers. What's the difference between an *escaper* and an *escapee? Payee* and *allottee* might be argued for, but what about *integree* or *playee* or *deceivee?*

ADVISORIAL,   whatever it is supposed to mean, is not an English word. It may be in error for *advisory.* Don't use it.

AFFECT, EFFECT   should never be confused, yet often are. *Affect* is always a verb, never a noun. It means "to influence" or "to have an effect on." *Effect* may be both a verb, meaning "to bring about," "to accomplish," or "to produce," and a noun meaning "result," "impression," "influence." You can *effect* a change in rules. In doing so you may *affect* the behavior of those who must obey the rules. The *effect* of the change may be good or bad. See **complement, compliment.**

AFFECTIVE   should be left to the professors who don't like simple words like *emotional. Since affective* can easily be confused with *effective* or *affection,* why use it at all?

AGGRAVATE   only colloquially means "to irritate" or "to exasperate." Its true meaning is "to make heavier" (from the Latin meaning exactly that), "to make worse," or "to make something more troublesome." You can *aggravate* a physical condition, such as a hernia, or a situation (i.e., "your attitude *aggravates* your offense"). Avoid the colloquial use. 57% of the Harper panel would use it only in the sense of "make worse" in their writing, but 53% might let the colloquial use slip into their speech.

AGREE ABOUT, TO, WITH   are all idioms with different meanings. You *agree about* a matter; you *agree to* a proposal; you *agree with* others of the same opinion.

AID AND ABET   is repetitious. Say "help."

AIN'T,   the bugbear of schoolmarms, has become the stigma of the illiterate or the careless. Let it rest in peace, but remember that "ain't I" has much more excuse for being than "aren't I" *(q.v.),* with the first person singular pronoun. "He ain't" and "you ain't" are always wrong.

9

ALGORITHM   is dandy for shoving off. Nobody, including you, will know what it means.

ALGY   is an abbreviation of algorithm: a concept in which a problem's solution is sought in a set of ordered steps or calculations. Computerese.

ALLOTTEE   See *advisee*. Unfortunately, most of the -ee words now have dictionary sanction. If you feel uneasy about some of the recent "improvements" in English, make a practice of consulting the Merriam Second Edition, published in 1934, before we decided that usage was our major criterion. The Random House *Dictionary of the English Language* goes overboard for usage less often than the Merriam Third, but it does include words like *abort* as a noun and *escapee* and *allottee*. In fact, according to the OED, *allottee* goes back to 1846, *escapee* to 1875. Nevertheless, you should resist the -ee, -ize, -wise habit. It's not wrong; it's just ugly.

ALL RIGHT   is two words, not one spelled "alright," even though we spell *already* and *altogether* as single words. 86% of the Harper panel rejected *alright*.

ALLUSION, ILLUSION.   This is another tricky pair of sound-alikes. They have no similarity in meaning. Using one for the other is an illiterate error. *Allusion* means a reference; *illusion* means a false idea or perception.

ALPHABET SOUP   is military slang for ABC: Atomic, Biological, and Chemical Warfare.

ALSO   See *Plus.*

ALTHOUGH, THOUGH   are in general interchangeable, though although usually begins a subordinate clause preceding a main clause and *though* begins a clause after a main clause, as in this sentence.

AMBIVALENT, AMBIGUOUS.   Newman says, "Ambivalent, which means having conflicting feelings—feelings, for example, of love and hate—is shoving *ambiguous,* which means uncertain or doubtful. *Ambiguous* should shove back."

AMMO   is CIA Talk for "Alert Memorandum, using the military abbreviation for ammunition to refer to secret documents warning of potential foreign crises.

10

AMONG, BETWEEN. Don't let the permitters make you a permitee (see *advisee)*. No matter how hard they strain to make these words interchangeable, they aren't. *Among* always refers to more than two persons or things; *between* is limited to two. "Between you and me and the gatepost," though now irreversibly idiomatic (and trite), is grammatically wrong since the confidence is among more than two. "Between you and me" is, of course, correct. "An agreement was drawn up between France, Italy, Sweden, and Great Britain" is wrong. The distinction may be weakening, but 72-78% of the Harper panel prefer to keep *between* between two and *among* among more than two.

AMONGST. Americans say *among*.

A.M., P.M. may be written a.m., p.m., always with periods showing that they are abbreviations. 12 M. indicates noon, 12 P.M. midnight. Don't say, "Tomorrow night at 10 P.M." or "Tuesday morning at 8 A.M." *P.M.* means after noon, *A.M.* before noon. You don't need both P.M. or A.M. *and* the words "night" and "morning."

ANALYZATION is not an honest word, even though the Third and Random House accept it, and the OED says that it goes back to 1742. The noun from the word *analyze* is *analysis.* Let's not loosely invent new words as replacements for already established words. See **orientate.**

AND ETC. is the result of sheer ignorance. The *et* of *et cetera* means "and."

AND/OR is a bastard construction, useful in lists, estimates, contracts, etc., but out of place in formal writing or speaking. Those who use it probably think of it as an efficient word-saver. They could better display their interest in verbal economy by cutting down inflated sentences and paragraphs.

ANYONE, ANYBODY, like *no one, nobody, nothing, everyone, everybody, somebody, some one, each,* are singular pronouns. "Will *everybody* raise *their* hand?" is wrong. "Their" should be "his" or "her." Only *none* can be both singular and plural.

APE, GOING is slang for erratic behavior. A subtle interpretation is that it is an acronym for "above political expediency."

11

APPLICABLE   at the time of MW2 could only be pronounced with the accent on the first syllable. Enough people have mispronounced it since then that the accent on "plic" is now acceptable, but only just. Say it *AP-lic-ab'l.*

APT, LIKELY, LIABLE   are *apt* to be confused. *Apt* and *likely,* when followed by an infinitive, are *likely* to be interchangeable in the sense of "probable" or "tending toward." *Apt* has another meaning, "quick to understand," "relevant" or "appropriate" as in "an apt pupil." *Liable* is in a different league. It is not an acceptable substitute for *likely* in "You are *liable* to get wet if you go out in the rain." Leave *liable* to the cops and lawyers: *"Liable* for damages," *"liable* to arrest."

AREA   is a perfectly good Latin word which orginally meant a level piece of ground. It is used far too often to mean, vaguely, almost any range, scope, extent, or field. "We're doing better in this area [race relations, religion, sports, etc., etc.]." Keep *area* geographical. Don't let it become a retreat from definiteness like *factor, facet,* and *along these lines.* The DOD *Dictionary* properly sticks to the geographical meaning of surface, tract, region, section, as in "area of interest," "area of operations," "area of war," "area command," "area control center," and "area of influence."

AREN'T I?   is a schoolma'am's coy way of avoiding *ain't I.* It is not only grammatically wrong but sick-making. If you haven't the guts to say *ain't I* (which is historically correct, though only in the first person singular) say *amn't I* or *am I not* or revise your sentence.

AROUND   in the sense of "approximately" is colloquial. *Around* and *round* are widely used as synonyms, though in formal writing only *around* is acceptable in the meanings: "in a circle," "on all sides," going in a circular route." "Around the world," not "round the world." *All-round* meaning "versatile" is preferable to *all-around.*

ARROGATE, ABROGATE   are an unlikely slippery pair. Their meanings are so far apart, 1. "appropriate to oneself arrogantly" and 2. "to abolish or cancel," that only a jackass will confuse them and say, "He abrogated to himself full power." In simple communication neither word is necessary.

ARTHRITIS.   Don't make it *"Arthuritis*

AS   is a poor substitute for *because* since it may confuse the reader. "I didn't hear the bell *as* I was mowing the lawn" may mean I didn't hear it because or at the time I was mowing the lawn. Use *since* or *because.*

AS IF, AS THOUGH   are interchangeable and may be followed by either a subjunctive ("were") or indicative ("was") form of the verb "to be." "He acts *as though* he *were* the owner" is no more correct these days than "He acts *as if* he *was* the owner," but those who love the language will still prefer "were."

ASSET   becomes an impersonal cover-all word that can refer to people, groups, relationships, instruments, installations, or supplies. Let *assets* be valuable or desirable things. When you talk about people, let them stay human and not limply exist as personnel or *assets.*

ATMOSPHERE   is an overused substitute for *environment* (also overused), which is made to do service for *area* (which can vaguely mean almost anything) instead of simply describing the "air that surrounds the earth" (DOD definition).

ATMOSPHERIC ENVIRONMENT.   For God's sake say *air.* Such constructions are intolerably pompous. Other examples: "aqueous environment," "missile environment," "limited combat environment." See *environment.*

ATTRIT   is a hideous derivation from *attrition* to form a bastard verb. *Attrite* is listed in the new dictionaries, but is not much better than *attrit,* and the OED mentions it only as an adjective, now obsolete. Cf. *liase* and *surveil.*

AUGMENT   means "to increase" or "enlarge." The military meaning of "add to" or "transfer to," as in "I was augmented into the regular Marine Corps" is a mysterious, unidiomatic usage.

AUSTERITY (of assets):   a pompous way to say "short of supplies or men."

AUTHOR   is a noun, not a verb.

BACHELORS,   meaning bachelor's degree. See **masters.**

BACK TO THE DRAWING BOARD   is a weary cliché for starting a project over after a failure. Sometimes replaced by "cold shower time."

BAD   is the proper predicate adjective after "feel." "I feel bad" is correct. You "feel badly" only when your sense of touch fails. Harper quotes Clifton Fadiman: "Don't feel bad when you hear the broadcaster say he feels badly. Just remember that all men are created equally."

BAFFLEGAB,   like GOBBLEDYGOOK, refers to jargon, especially that intended to confuse rather than to enlighten.

BALISAGE   is a beautiful word that deserves recognition, though it appears in no English dictionary except that of the DOD. It means "the marking of a route by a system of dim beacon lights enabling vehicles to be used at near day-time speed, under blackout conditions." In French it means the setting of buoys or beacons. The military have taken over a number of words from other languages *(parlimentaire, reclama)* which have no present place in English dictionaries.

BALL GAME,   as in "It's a whole new ball game," is a cliché. Let others wear it out.

BALLISTICALLY INDUCED APERTURES IN THE CUTANEOUS ENVIRONMENT   means "bullet wounds." The gobbledygook doesn't even sound better than the translation.

BALLPARK FIGURE,   meaning a rough estimate, once a colorful metaphor, has become a cliché.

BARBITURATE   should have the accent on the TYOOR syllable, but most people put it on BITCH. Both pronunciations are now acceptable. Be sure you don't lose the final "r" sound.

BASED ON   often becomes a dangling participle. Be sure that it has a noun to modify, as "His accuracy as a marksman was based on practice." "Based on practice, he was a good marksman" is incorrect.

BASIC FUNDAMENTALS.   What's the difference between *basic* and *fundamental?* It must sound impressive because so many people use it.

BASIS   is a Latin word whose plural is *basēs.* Don't confuse it with the plural of *base,* which has the same spelling but different pronunciation. And don't let a little Latin go to your head so that you make the plural *basises.* Other words like *basis,* whose plurals change the final vowel to long *ē,* are *thesis, crisis,* and *diagnosis.* Don't give them an extra syllable, and don't try to show off by pronouncing a standard English word like *processes* with a long final *ē.*

14

BEAT is not an acceptable past participle of *beat.* "I feel *beat*" is as illiterate as "We drug it down the road," or "I'm all shook up."

BECAUSE. See **as.**

BENEFICIATE may be a good word for iron smelters, but it is a ridiculous error for *benefit.*

BETWEEN A ROCK AND A HARD PLACE is a worn-out and not very clever metaphor.

BETWEEN, AMONG. See **among.**

BETWEEN...TO, as in "between 58 to 62 degrees," is a faulty idiom. It should be *between* 58 *and* 62 degrees."

BIMONTHLY AND SEMIMONTHLY are listed as synonyms by most dictionaries, following ignorant usage, which makes *bimonthly* mean both every two months and twice a month. Since we already have *semimonthly* to mean twice a month, why allow *bimonthly* to become ambiguous? It should mean, exclusively, every two months.

BIOFEEDBACK is computerese for programming that teaches conscious control of heartbeat, blood-pressure, etc.

BIT, meaning "specialty" or "distinctive behavior," as in "She does the Lady Bountiful bit whenever she can," is not in good usage. 68% of the Harper panel disapprove of it in writing, but about the same number wouldn't mind using it in casual speech.

BITCH as a noun applied to human females is vulgar slang. As a verb meaning "to complain" it is ordinary slang, as is *bitch up,* meaning "to mess up," "bungle."

BITE THE BULLET is the manly equivalent of "face the music," used *ad nauseam* during the early days of President Ford's administration. Some lovers of clichés like the idea of courage it suggests by the image of a wounded soldier in the days before anesthesia, given a lead bullet to bite while he endured surgery.

BLACK is now preferred to *Negro* among blacks.

BLEND WORDS like *brunch, smog,* and *chortle,* combinations of two words to form a third (*brunch* = breakfast and lunch), are part of language development. *Guesstimate* and *happenstance* are still a little nauseating to purists, but will probably survive.

15

BLOC   should not ignorantly be spelled *block.*

BOAT, SHIP   should be differentiated. Navy men make the distinction that a *boat* is any waterborne vessel small enough to be lifted aboard a ship. Submarines, however are *boats,* as are *canoes, rowing shells, landing craft, etc.*

BOGGLE,   as in "the mind boggles at . . . ," is a popular cliché. Leave it to the columnists.

BOMFOG   is an acronym for "Brotherhood of Man, Fatherhood of God," said of bombastic speech.

BONA FIDE.   Though permissive dictionaries now allow and even prefer *bonafide* (to rhyme with *tide*), you can show respect for a fine phrase borrowed from the Latin, meaning "in good faith," by making the second word rhyme with *tidy.*

BOOBOO   is slang for silly error. It doesn't yet belong in formal communication.

BOONDOCKS, BOONIES   are military slang words (from Tagalog *bundok,* mountain), made popular by Marines after the Spanish-American War. They expressively describe the back country, the "sticks." Like *hassle* and *rip-off, boondocks* will probably become standard English.

BOTTOM LINE   is a dubious product of the 70s, meaning something like "the last word," or "the final reckoning." It is especially obnoxious when used as a verb. Like "tough it out," "stonewall," and "point in time," it is tainted by Watergate.

BRAINSTORM   is really two words, describing a mental disturbance or, one word, a sudden inspiration. The bright people who like to invent new words came up with *brainstorming,* now listed in most dictionaries as a conference technique in which a group solves problems by unrestrained, spontaneous discussion. *Brainstorm,* the verb from *brainstorming,* is listed only in MW3.

BRASS,   originally military slang for "high-ranking officers," is now common in civilian slang as well, though the gold braid and "scrambled eggs" of military insignia, which originally suggested the word, may be missing.

BRIEF. Can't we sometimes "discuss with," "address," or just "inform" or "talk to" a group or person instead of always *briefing* them? As a noun *brief* has a legal connotation. Avoid constructions like "give him a brief on the flight plan."

In another sense, the word might serve as a reminder to writers and speakers: *be* brief. Far too many briefings are not brief.

BRING, TAKE should be differentiated, but often are not. "Bring that book over to me" is correct, as is "Take this book over to that table." *Bring* involves transportation of something from a distance to the speaker; *take* means to transport it away from the speaker. 91% of the Harper panel observe the distinction in their writing, 84% in their speech.

BROWNNOSE is a particularly revolting slang verb meaning, for obvious reasons, "to curry favor," "apple-polish."

BUG in the sense of "irritate" is slang. 71% of the Harper panel would not use it in their writing, but 83% would use it in casual speech. *Bug* as a noun meaning a device for eavesdropping is in general informal use, as is *bug,* a verb meaning "to wiretap." Both usages are still strictly informal.

BUREAUCRATIZATION. What a lot of outrages are committed by the suffixes -ize, -wise, -ee, and -ation! You may be linguistically justified when you form nouns from verbs or make nouns and adjectives into overweight nouns by adding suffixes. Monstrosities like *bureaucratization* and *civilianization, however,* are offenses against the language. Naturally, the new dictionaries say they are all right. The OED wouldn't touch *bureaucratization* with a bargepole and calls *civilianization* a nonce word. That's what we should call a lot of words these days.

BURGEON means "to bud," not "to proliferate" or "grow rapidly."

BURGLE, a verb deriving from burglar (like "liaise" from "liaison"), is now, alas, acceptable. We have better words for the same thing. How do you like "buttle" from "butler"? Same process!

BUT, HOWEVER are very useful transitional conjunctions *(however* is usually a simple adverb, but often becomes a conjunction when it introduces an independent clause). They should be sparingly used to begin sentences. *However* as a conjunction is preceded by a semicolon, *but* by a comma. A composition through which are scattered *howevers* at the beginning of many sentences is amateurish.

BUY   is a verb, not a noun. "Buy me a drink," when none is for sale, is an overused cliché. "A good buy" is slang.

BUZZ WORDS   are the basic ingredients of gobbledygook *(q.v.)*. New World gives one definition of *buzz* as "a confused sound, as of many excited voices," which precisely describes words like *interface, oversight,* and *parameter.*

CADRE   is usually pronounced KAD-rē by the military. The Random House prefers kad'r. Since most people don't know what a *cadre* really means, you would be kind to use a simpler word, like *framework* or *unit.*

CAMOUFLET   is a military word taken from the French. The DOD *Dictionary* limits its meaning to "the resulting cavity in a deep underground burst when there is no rupture of the surface." Webster's Third gives it a wider meaning: a *camouflet* is a mine intended to destroy enemy mining tunnels or a subsurface explosion that leaves a sealed pocket of smoke and gas. Its original meaning in French is "smoke blown in a sleeper's face from lighted paper." *There's* a word for you! The OED traces it back to 1836 in its military meaning of a mine placed in a wall of earth between besieged and besieger, whose explosion will bury or suffocate or cut off the retreat of the sapper on the opposite side. It is pronounced kam-o-flā.

CAMP adj.,   is popular slang to describe something so out of fashion that it has become fashionable again, like 20s clothes, Tiffany lamps.

CANNOT HELP BUT   is grammatically indefensible, a double negative, even though many people use it. Leave out the *but* and use a participle. It isn't as bad as "can't hardly," but it isn't good either.

CAPABILITY.   There's nothing wrong with this sturdy word except that it gets used so often that it begins to sound like an echo: "forward aspect engagement capability," "maximum operational capability," "support capability," "search capability." The DOD *Dictionary* nicely clouds the precise definition of *capability,* "the ability to execute a specified course of action," by adding "may or may not be accompanied by an intention." Often it is only a pompous way of saying "ability."

CARE LESS,COULD (NOT)   See **could care less.**

18

CARIBBEAN   has acquired the pronunciation with the accent on -ib, though *Car-i-BE-en* is preferred.

CATCH 22   is a popular reference to a novel satirizing war, published in 1962 by Joseph Heller. If you use it to describe an idea or a situation, be sure you know what you are talking about. It means something that depends upon something else, which in turn depends upon the first thing: a stalemate.

CAVALRY, CALVARY   shouldn't be confused but often are. Some not very observant Americans tend to put their horsemen on the Mount of Skulls.

CAVEAT   is a rather pedantic synonym for "warning." It should be a noun, though it is often made into a verb, sanctioned by the Merriam Dictionaries, as in "The General caveated that there'll be some changes around here." Random House and American Heritage make it only a noun. The OED says that the verb goes back to 1661. They abused the language in those days too. If you must use it as a verb, keep it intransitive. You can't *caveat* somebody or -bodies. The word is the third person singular, present subjunctive form of the Latin verb *cavere*, "to beware," and literally means "let him beware." You can, if you insist, even speak of a *caveatee*. Please don't.

CENTER AROUND   is a silly metaphor. Centers don't circle. Say *center in.*

CHAIRPERSON   is a concession to militant women, who don't know that the primary meaning of *man* is "a person, whether male or female." Let's not pervert the language to prevent so-called sexist bias by creating monstrosities like "spokesperson," "personkind," etc., avoiding fine, strong words like "humanity," just because they have *man* in them. What will the ladies do with *"woman"?* The 1980 edition of the OED does not list *chairperson.*

CHAISE LONGUE   is a French phrase meaning "long chair," *not* "lounge chair." The correct pronunciation is shaz or shez long, not "chase lounge," even though Merriam Third, taking the popular, uninformed vote, says both are acceptable.

CHOW,   still considered slang in the meaning of "food," as in a *chow* line, is listed by Random House as short for *chow-chow,* which it calls pidgin English for a kind of Chinese preserve or any mixed food, food in general, or a meal. MW2 also says it's pidgin English, but makes it a derivation of *chow mein ch'ao,* meaning "to fry, and *mein,* "flour," in Pekinese Chinese. That word *ch'ao* sounds like a very respectable ancestor for *chow*—not pidgin English.

CHUTZPAH   is a splendid Yiddish word which only just made it to the Merriam Third new-word section. It means gall or extreme self-confidence. Pronounce it KUTZ-pah or HUTTS-pah, not TCHUTZ-pah.

CIRCUMVENT, CIRCUMSCRIBE   are far enough apart in meaning ("surround by trickery" or "prevent" and "encircle or limit") so that no one should confuse them. Yet, under Tresidder's Law, any word, however clear in meaning, will on occasion be foolishly misused.

CIVILIANIZATION   is another barbarism like *bureaucratization (q.v.).* MW3 says both are acceptable. That's too bad.

CLICHÉ   is a French word meaning a stereotype plate for printing. It is better known as the word to describe a phrase that has been repeated so often that it has become hackneyed: "last but not least," "knee-high to a grasshopper," "pretty as a picture," "bored to tears."

CLIMATE   *of opinion* (or anything else not associated with the weather) is a cliché.

CLIQUE   can be pronounced either KLEEK or CLICK, according to permissive dictionaries, which also allow KREEK and KRICK for *creek.* Those who know any French will prefer KLEEK.

CLOSE BUT NO CIGAR   is a cliché from carnival slang that is almost CAMP. A contemporary equivalent is "Near-Miss-ile."

CLOUT   is a current "in-word" with the gobbledygook specialists. Like *spectrum* and *escalate* and *posture* and *viable* it will go out of style, and some other smart word will replace it for the next cycle of bureaucratic clichés. *Clout* is an Anglo-Saxon word meaning "lump of earth" which baseball fans adopted to describe a good hit by a bat. Except in the sport of archery, where it means a target or a hit in the target, the word is listed in many dictionaries as archaic, dialectic, colloquial, or slang. The MW3 thinks it's O.K. Try not to agree.

CLUTCH   is one of those clichés, like *clout, escalate, spectrum, orchestrate, nitty-gritty,* which bureaucrats like to use frequently, under the mistaken impression that they thereby make the language colorful and vigorous. It is slang for "emergency" or "critical situation."

20

COADUNATE is a very impressive Latin adjective meaning "united" or "joined together." Unless you want your audience to admire your vocabulary, be satisfied with "united." This is just the kind of show-off word that could slip into verb form, and, sure enough, the MW3 says it can. Leave it to the biologists.

COGNITIVE, like *cognizance,* is academic gobbledygook, having to do with knowledge or perception. When used in combination with vague words like "recognition" and "domain," it is highly objectionable.

COGNIZANCE is the stuffed-shirt or legal substitute for "knowledge," "notice," "jurisdiction," "awareness." When you're tempted to say *take cognizance of,"* for "notice" or "officially recognize," resist and use the simpler words.

COHESE, like *attrit, liase,* and *surveil,* is a back-formation from a noun, in this case *cohesion.* Only the linguistically insensitive would use it.

COHORT comes from the Latin word for a Roman military unit of from 300 to 600 men, one tenth of a legion. Since MW2, which gave it a strictly military meaning, it has come to mean "followers," "companions," "associates." Be sure you don't speak of one person as a *cohort.* Most of the Harper panel prefer the military meaning in their writing, but would use *cohorts* in its sense of "band of associates" in their speech.

COLLECTIVE NOUNS are singular in form but describe a group of people, animals, or things: *jury, family, herd, couple.* They take singular verbs when they are considered units: "Her family was present at the ceremony." They take plural verbs when they are regarded as collections of individuals: "Her family are all highstrung people."

COMBAT INTEGRITY sounds great, but is usually fuzzy.

COMMENCE is a rather stuffy synonym for "begin."

COMMENTATE is another misbegotten word like *analyzation.* It is a verb derived from the noun "commentator," one who *commentates* rather than *comments* on the news. Stand by the basic word. We don't need *commentate.*

COMMONALITY   is an alternate spelling of *commonalty*, listed in MW 2 and 3, but not in Random House or New World, meaning "ordinary people as distinguished from those with authority or rank." Only MW3 defines it as what appears to be an arbitrary distortion of the original meaning to "possession with another of a certain attribute," "commonness." This is another example of uninformed usage depriving a valid word of the real meaning.

COMMUTE TO AND FROM WORK   is redundant since *commute* covers both directions. Say "commute to work."

COMPARATIVES   must be completed. You can't say that some one is taller or a product is cheaper or a radio station carries more news unless you tell what they are taller or cheaper than and what stations carry less news.

COMPARE   is a tricky word. You *compare* one thing or person *to* another when they are essentially similar; when there may be differences as well as similarities, you usually *compare* them *with* each other: "This house is cheap compared to that one." "Compare this picture with that in the Tate Gallery."

COMPARE, CONTRAST.   You *compare* like things, which may have some dissimilarities, but *contrast* things which are essentially different. A lady might be poetically compared to a summer's day, but the day itself contrasts sharply with a winter's day. You *compare* like things *to* each other, emphasizing similarity; you *compare* them *with* each other if the emphasis is on dissimilarity. The verb *contrast* is followed by *with*. The noun can be followed by *between*, "*contrast between* two people," and we speak of things being in *contrast to* each other.

COMPLEMENT, COMPLIMENT,   like *effect* and *affect, principle* and *principal, apprise* and *appraise, allusion* and *illusion, imminent* and *eminent, respectively* and *respectfully, marital* and *martial, incredible* and *incredulous,* are often confused. Look them up. They don't give much trouble as nouns, but as verbs they constantly get in each other's way. *Complement* means to complete or make perfect; *compliment* means to praise.

COMPTROLLER   is a variant of *controller* and should be pronounced without any -mp sound, exactly like *controller*.

COMPUTERESE is the esoteric language of those who serve the new god, the computer. It is full of invented, high-sounding words which seem to have meaning for those of the true faith, but are baffling to all others: *micrologic, neural-dynamic, to access, preformatted, hyperquadratic, cyber-cultural, systems analysis, content-addressable, data* as a singular noun.

CONCEPT means idea. It is all too often used as an impressive label for a run-of-the-mill plan or a nebulous generalized notion.

CONCEPTUALIZE. Whoever invented this pompous verb was no doubt pleased with himself. He had no reason to be. It's in American dictionaries, with lofty meanings, not in the OED.

CONCRETIZE is one of the more unpleasant -ize words. Put it with *optimize, cosmetize, civilianize, prioritize, conceptualize,* and *finalize* and set fire to them.

CONFIDENTIALITY took a beating during the Watergate hearings. It's a correct but pretentious word.

CONFIGURATION is no improvement over "design" or "form," but probably sounds more professional. Aviators love it.

CONGERIES is an old and rather fussy word meaning a pile or collection of things, events, ideas, etc. which has given way to progress and can be (should be, according to Random House) pronounced kon-JIR-ēz rather than kon-JIR-i-ēz because most users don't know any better. Why use it at all?

CONGRATULATION, too often pronounced "congradulation," is sometimes foolishly spelled that way.

CONSENSUS should not be followed by "of opinion." It does very well by itself. *General consensus* is also tautological.

CONSORTIUM should be pronounced *con-SOR-shee-em* (though MW 3 has bowed to the ignorant and accepted *-ti-um*). Why do we have to use it at all? *Partnership* or *association* says the same thing.

CONSTRAINT is a respectable word meaning "restriction" or "compulsion" that has fallen into low company and became addictive. No budget is complete without having *constraints.* Try to kick the habit.

23

CONTACT as a verb meaning "get in touch with" has shouldered its way into dictionaries, though it still jars on many lovers of the language. Use it if you must, but not with the lovers. 65% of the Harper panel reject it in writing, but 63% use it in casual speech.

CONTACT-MAKING is a military euphemism for fighting a battle. Contacting the enemy avoids mention of lack of success.

CONTAINERIZATION is another ugly new word which MW3 hasn't yet discovered (only Random House has). Unhappily, it's all over the place. Harper says it's among the least objectionable of the -ize words.

CONTAMINIZE. How we love to play around with -ize! There is no such word. For a wonder, even the Merriam Third doesn't recognize it. Try *contaminate.*

CONTINUOUS, CONTINUAL. The new dictionaries have hopelessly fouled up these words, which once had useful distinctions. Now they are interchangeable, though the purists say *continuous* when something goes on without a break, *continual* when something recurs repeatedly.

CONVINCE, PERSUADE are not synonyms, though even some good writers think that they can "*convince* people to do something." We are *persuaded to* act or think; we are *convinced of* something. We may be *convinced* that something is true, but we are *persuaded,* not *convinced,* to believe it.

COPACETIC is U. S. slang old enough to be listed in MW1 as a smart synonym for "capital, snappy, prime." Now Random House still calls it slang, but "capital" and "snappy" have been replaced by "fine" and "O.K."

COP OUT is slang, new since 1961, for backing out of an unwanted responsibility. *Cop-out* is the noun. It should not be used in formal writing.

COPE as in "The employee who gets this assignment must be able to *cope,*" which does not say what he has to cope with, is unacceptable in formal writing, though common in casual speech.

CORRIGENDUM. Why use the gerundive of a Latin word, "that which should be corrected," when the word "error" will do? If you must use it and want a nice heading for a list of corrections, be sure you give it the proper Latin plural, *corrigenda.*

COSMETIC   is a recent addition to bureaucratic gobbledygook, an adjective figuratively meaning "prettied up" or improved in appearance." Leave it to the makers of lipstick.

COST-EFFECTIVE   is bureaucratese for "economical" or "money-saving." It is not listed, even in MW 3, but is habit-forming, as are ugly derivatives like *costing out.*

COULD (COULD NOT) CARE LESS   is an overworked hyperbole. The proper phrase, of course, is "could not care less," if you must use it. Without the negative it makes no sense.

COUNTER-   is a prefix much admired by the military. The DOD *Dictionary* lists twenty words preceded by *counter,* only one of them, for some reason, as two separate words: *counter air.* It does not list *counterproductive,* a favorite of diplomats, but comes up with one of the longest words in the language, *counterreconnaissance.* Let's not overdo it with inventions like *counterbattery.* What's the matter with "opposing battery?"

COUNTERPRODUCTIVE   is popular gobbledygook for "self-defeating," "unwise," misguided." It doesn't even sound good. Newman calls it a "new cliché," which has already spawned a medical monstrosity, "countertherapeutic."

COUPLE   is a noun, not an adjective. "I took a couple aspirin" is wrong. Say "couple of..."

CREATIVE ETHNICITY   is typical of formal gobbledygook. What does it really mean?

CREDENTIALIZING   is beyond the pale, as is *credential* used as a verb.

CREDIBLE   means believable. Don't confuse it with *credulous,* ready to believe, or *creditable,* worthy of credit, esteem, or belief.

CRITERIA   is a Greek plural. The singular is *criterion.*

CRITICAL   has several different meanings. Use it carefully. It causes little trouble when it is a synonym for crucial or refers to a critic's analysis, good or bad. But don't say that a person is *critical* when he is in hospital in poor condition. His condition is *critical;* he isn't.

CRITIQUE   is a noun, not a verb. Since most military officers are taught "to critique" papers, briefings, lecturers, etc., however, they will not be stopped by the proper function of a part of speech. Only MW3 recognizes it as a verb. Better verbs are "criticize," "review," "analyze," "comment on," "evaluate." At least they're real verbs. The OED notes that *critique* was used as a verb as far back as 1751, but that doesn't make it good. 87-93% of the Harper panel reject it as a verb in both speech and writing.

CRUNCH,   like *flap, clout,* and *thrust,* is a bureaucratic vogue word, meaning "a critical situation, particularly a financial one." If you "come down to the *crunch,*" you've reached a moment of decision.

CRYPTIC   means "secret" or "mysterious." The meaning of "brief" is a recent and not very precise addition.

CULTURE,   according to the DOD *Dictionary,* is "features of the terrain that have been constructed by men. Included are such items as roads, buildings, and canals; boundary lines, and, in a broad sense, all names and legends on a map." There must be some military leaders who give this word a broader meaning.

CUSTOMIZE   is -ize gobbledygook seized upon as legitimate by MW3 (though other dictionaries ignore it). It means to build, fit, or alter to a customer's specifications as "to *customize* an automobile or hair-style." It is perhaps more palatable than *strategize, sectorize,* and *prioritize,* but is best left to barbers and tailors.

CUT THE MUSTARD   is an odd phrase which for some reason not literally apparent means "to be successful," "to be well qualified." It is still not suitable for formal writing, though it has been in use since at least the time of O. Henry.

DANGLING ELEMENTS   are usually participles which modify the wrong word, e.g., "Reading the paper, my toast burned" or " Going in on Route 50, the Iwo Jima Memorial is on your right." The toast isn't reading, of course; neither is the Memorial mobile. Infinitives can also dangle: "To avoid embarrassment, the door should be locked." Make sure that the subject of the main clause modified by the participle or infinitive is the right one: "Reading the paper, I burned the toast." "To avoid embarrassment, you should lock the door." Shifting the verb of the main clause into the passive voice often causes awkward danglers. Watch your participles. They can easily booby-trap you.

26

DASHES AND OTHER FLAMBOYANT PUNCTUATION. See **ellipses.**

DATA is a Latin plural. The singular, in spite of computer specialists, is *datum*. *Data* always takes a plural verb. Until the next round of dictionaries, "the data is" is wrong. It's slipping, however: only 51% of the Harper panel refuse to use it as a singular in writing, and 65% say it aloud, damn it! See **media.**

DAYLIGHT SAVING TIME is right. "Daylight savings time" is wrong because *savings* is a noun, and the phrase needs an adjective.

DEADLINE for most of us means a time limit for a news story or a payment. It originally meant a line around a prison beyond which a prisoner could not go without risk of being shot. For the military it means "a group of vehicles put aside for maintenance" or, as a verb, "to put vehicles aside for maintenance or repair." It is so recorded only by MW3. Civilian readers are likely to be puzzled by the military use.

DÉBUT See **première.**

DECIMATE literally means "to kill one in ten." Don't use it loosely to mean "totally destroy." And don't apply it to inanimate objects. 86% of the Harper panel reject its use except in the meaning of "to destroy a large part of a group."

DECISION is a noun, never a verb, except possibly in boxing.

DECISIONAL is gobbledygook. See **decision.**

DEDICATE means "to set apart for a special purpose, devote to some work, duty, etc." Use it carefully: one may be *devoted* to a person or an idea or work, but *dedicated* only to an idea or work, not to a person.

DEFEAT. You can *defeat* an enemy, but not an aircraft or other inanimate object.

DEGRADE means "to lower in rank or status," "to bring into dishonor or contempt," or "to lower in value, price, or quality." The military has its own special meaning for it, not necessarily, as in *augment* and *discrepancy,* in accord with the commonly accepted meaning: "to reduce," applied to things or qualities or situations rather than to people. "Our capability was degraded because of discrepancies in our weapons," "degradation of mobility," "degradation of speed by wind resistance." This is not standard usage.

27

DELETE means to erase or cross out a word or letter. Military usage boldly extends the meaning to include troops, aircraft, etc. They don't simply *eliminate* a battery of howitzers. They *delete* it. Leave it to the proof-readers.

DÉMARCHE is diplomatic gobbledygook for a step forward in international tactics.

DEPART should be an intransitive verb, which cannot take an object. You should *depart from* Louisville, not *depart* Louisville. Up to MW3 (1961) the transitive use was marked archaic, as in "depart this life."

DEPLOY. Can't the military sometimes *go* to or *leave* a place instead of always *deploying?* The DOD *Dictionary* meaning is more restrictive: to *deploy* is "1. to relocate forces to desired areas of operations," "2. to extend or widen the front of a military unit," or "3. to change from a cruising approach or contact disposition [whatever that is] to a disposition for naval battle."

DEPRECATE AND DEPRECIATE are a slippery pair. They are *not* interchangeable. *Deprecate* (L., to pray against) means "to express disapproval of" something or somebody. *Depreciate* (L., to lower the price) means to belittle or lessen in value. MW3 says that they are synonyms, admitting that their similarity in spelling has influenced the confusion. Keep them apart.

DESTABILIZE is a disgraceful euphemism used during the early 70s as a nice way of saying "corrupt" and "undermine," as in CIA operations *destabilizing* the Communist government of Chile.

DESTRUCT is another ridiculous, unnecessary verb formed from a noun. Unfortunately for the future of the language, television has immortalized the nauseating phrase "to self-destruct," and the new dictionaries admit it as a verb. Stick to "destroy."

DIALOGUE used to mean the passages of talk in a play or story or, simply, a conversation. It has been diplomatically upgraded to describe what goes on in the Oval Office, usually a "constructive or meaningful dialogue," or any discussion between important officials, even when it is largely a *monologue* by one of them. *Discussion* or *conversation* is better. A bureaucrat once defined *dialogue* as "a meaningful initiative followed by a constructive response." Poppycock!

DICHOTOMY, any division into two parts, has become a cliché. When it's turned into a verb and back into a noun, in *dichotomization,* it's a monstrosity, even though you can find authority for it.

DIFFERENT FROM is the accepted American idiom, but *different than* is creeping up on it, especially when the phrase is followed by a clause: "Your way of speaking is different than it used to be." Precise writers will avoid the correct but awkward form, "different from what it used to be," by recasting the sentence: "Your speech has changed."

DIPHTHERIA should be so spelled and pronounced dif-THEER-ee-ah because the ph letter in Greek has an f, not a p sound. Because most people, including doctors, don't know any Greek (though they say "Phi" in "Phi Beta Kappa" with the f sound), dictionaries now sanction the error and allow dip-THEER -ee-uh.

DISADVANTAGED, especially as applied to children, is educationese for "not bright" or "delinquent."

DISASTEROUS is not the proper spelling or pronunciation of *disastrous.*

DISCREDIT, which means "to disbelieve" or "cast doubt on something or somebody" or "disgrace," cannot be used in the sense of *penalize.*

DISCREET, DISCRETE may sound alike, but they are far apart. *Discreet,* a good, strong word, means "prudent," "careful;" *discrete,* a pretentious word, means "separate," "unrelated."

DISCREPANCY means a disagreement, difference, or inconsistency. The military use it, without logical justification, to mean "fault," "error," "failure," as in "The aircraft crashed because of engine discrepancies." Don't stretch a good word.

DISESTABLISH is euphemistic gobbledygook which covers the voluntary closing down of a position, getting the hell out, or involuntary destruction of the position. In business gobbledygook it may mean firing an employee.

DISINFORMATION is jargon for something generally true, but which leads to false conclusions.

DISINTERESTED   means "impartial," "unbiased," "not influenced by personal interest or selfish motives." Unfortunately, ignorant, incorrect usage as "uninterested" has gained it acceptance under that meaning in some dictionaries. Others have the grace to call such usage colloquial. To destroy the usefulness of *disinterested* by making it ambiguous is a linguistic shame. 91% of the Haper panel, bless their hearts, still observe the distinction.

DIVE   is a regular verb, whose principal parts are *dive, dived, dived*. The irregular past tense *dove*, however, is now accepted as standard English, even though a few die-hards hold out against it. *Dived* is still better than *dove*.

DOCTRINE   takes on overtones of "ultimate truth" in military usage, beyond its basic meaning of "principles taught and advocated by its believers." The DOD *Dictionary* calls it "the fundamental principles by which the military forces or elements thereof guide their actions in support of national objectives." It adds the nice qualification that accepted doctrine "is authoritative but requires judgment in action." So powerful a word should not be lightly—or too frequently—used.

DOOBIES: a slangy acronym for "Data Bases," information forming the foundation of computer programs. It is also technocratic slang for life itself. A fouled-up computer program is a "screwby doobie."

DO YOUR OWN THING,   though possibly from respectable antecedents, is today an inane cliché which we hope has not long to live in smart usage.

DOUBT THAT   is greatly to be preferred to *doubt if* in sentences like "He doubts if the bill will pass." *Doubt whether* is always correct in such constructions.

DOWN THE PIKE   is a cliché that needs freshening.

DRAG   is a regular verb whose principal parts are *drag, dragged, dragged*. The illiterate distortion of the past tense to *drug* is deplorable.

DRIVE UP THE WALL   is a slang cliché. Avoid it.

DROWN.   A person was *drowned*, not *was drownded*. The past tense is pronounced DRAUND, not DRAUND-ED.

30

DUE TO   is correct only when *due* is an adjective, modifying a specific noun: "His late arrival was due to an accident"; "The cancellation of mess night is due to circumstances beyond our control." Its use as an adverb is always wrong: "He came in late, due to an accident." "Due to circumstances beyond our control, the mess night has been cancelled." Since you may not have time to figure out whether *due* is an adjective or an adverb, you'd be wise to forget the phrase and use "because of," "on account of," or "since" in its place. Only the undiscriminating MW3 accepts the adverbial use, incorrectly calling it prepositional. 84% of the American Heritage Usage panel rejected the adverbial use as unacceptable in writing.

DUMB,   meaning "stupid," has no place in formal writing. *Dumb* should keep its true meaning of "speechless," though we probably can't get rid of "dumb bunny" and "dumb cluck."

EACH AND EVERY   is a tautological cliché. *Each* is enough.

ECHELON.   There's nothing wrong with this word, except that it is too often loosely used as a synonym for "level," "group," or "organization." It should stay precise as a subdivision of a combat force or a formation.

ECONOMICS, ECONOMICAL.   The "e" of the first syllable may be pronounced either ee or eh.

EDUCATIONESE   is the gobbledygook of school teachers and administrators. It is full of pompous, Latinized abstractions and preposterous euphemisms: *Conferencing, remediation, effectuate, programmatic thrust, psychomotor domain, optimal synthesis, underachiever, behavioral objectives, matrifocal family, maxigroups in a state of cognitive inertia.*

-EE ENDINGS   are all over the place. They are valid in words like *grantee, refugee, repartee,* and *trustee,* but too often become strained means of turning other parts of speech into awkward nouns, e.g., *rapee, standee, washee.* The Harper panel of consultants on usage split on acceptance of *escapee* for "fugitive." Far more than half rejected it in writing, but 66% admitted using it in speech.

EFFECT.   See **affect.**

EFFECTUATE   is dull swank for "bring about," "accomplish." Don't use it.

31

EITHER, NEITHER   are used with singular verbs: "Either Bill or Jack is coming." The first syllable of both words may be pronounced $\bar{e}$ or $\bar{i}$, though $\bar{e}$ is normal in most American speech.

ELDER, ELDEST   are often misused. You speak of the *elder* of two, the *eldest* of more than two. The same distinction applies to *older* and *oldest* and *younger* and *youngest*.

ELICIT, ILLICIT.   Another tricky pair. See *complement*. *Elicit* is always a verb meaning "to draw out"; *illicit* is an adjective meaning "unlawful." Confusion of the two words is just plain ignorance.

ELLIPSES,   the three dots that signify omission of words or words, usually in quotations, should not be too often used as interruptions in sentences. The same could be said for *dashes,* unnecessary underscoring, fluttery exclamation points, and ooh-and-ah over-capitalization to put excitement into communication. The result is a kind of coy diary style.

EMIGRATE, IMMIGRATE   fool many people. *Emigrate* means to leave one country to live in another; *immigrate* means to enter the new country: "He emigrated from Sweden"; "He immigrated to the United States."

EMOTE   is an unacceptable verb, backformed from *emotion.* Forget it.

ENCLOSED PLEASE FIND   is an obsolete letter-writer's cliché. If something is enclosed, the reader will find it. Say "I am enclosing. . ."

ENDEAVOR   is a fine word made pompous by those who always *endeavor,* never simply *try.*

ENORMITY, ENORMOUSNESE   are a slippery pair. *Enormity* is a grave offense against decency, right, or order, something outrageous or evil. It should not be confused with *enormousness,* which means large size. 69% of the Harper panel reject *enormousness* as a synonym of *enormity.*

EN ROUTE.   Two words, not one. Don't let *en* become *in.* It's a French phrase meaning "on the way."

ENSURE, INSURE.   Both spellings are correct. The military seem to prefer "ensure." "Insure" has wider currency.

32

ENTHUSE   is a back-formation from *enthusiasm* (like *liaise* from *liaison*). It is still regarded as colloquial—and a bit vulgar—in spite of the efforts of some lexicographers to make it respectable.

ENTROPY   is computerese for the amount of disorder in a system. It is properly a thermodynamic word, meaning a degree of sameness or similarity or the dissipation of energy into waste. Leave it to engineers.

ENVELOPE   as a noun should be pronounced ĕn-velope, not on-velope. Don't let a phony French first syllable show up your ignorance of this and other en- words, like *envoy, entry, enclave.* MW3 may give you permission to abuse some of the words. Ignore it.

ENVIRONMENT.   A great word when it has its primary meaning of "surroundings." Don't let it become a wordy abstraction. See **atmospheric environment** and **unsurvivable environment.**

ENVISION, ENVISAGE   are loosely used as synonyms, and MW3 unfortunately sanctions the usage. *Envision* means to imagine something not yet in existence (as "to *envision* a bright future"); *envisage* means to face (as "to *envisage* truth") or to visualize. Simpler words meaning the same things will prevent confusion.

ERR,   which by logical analogy with *error* should be pronounced "air," is supposed to be pronounced "uhr," according to most dictionaries. No one will think you are illiterate if you rhyme *err* with *pear.* Both Random House and American Heritage say both are acceptable, preferring "uhr" to "air."

ESCALATE   and *escalation* are tired words. Let them rest.

ESCAPE,   when it means physically getting away from something, must be followed by *from,* as "escape from prison," not "escape prison." *From* is not required when the word is used figuratively, meaning "to avoid successfully," as in "She wanted to escape his harsh words."

ESCHATOLOGY,   a fine, resonant, two-dollar word meaning the study of final things like death and taxes, has nothing to do with *scatology,* the study of or obsession with feces (for which there's a better four-letter word). Don't confuse them.

ESPECIALLY, SPECIALLY   should be differentiated. *Specially* indicates that an action is taken for a definite reason, as in "specially selected wines," "specially selected for an assignment." *Especially* means "to a marked degree" or "particularly," as in "He is an especially fine officer," "I came especially because it's your birthday." *"Especial* and *special* are generally interchangeable, though *special* is far more common.

ESSENTIAL,   like *unique* and *perfect,* cannot be compared. Nothing can be *more essential* than something else. *Most essential,* however, is correct, emphasizing the importance of something in itself, without comparing it to something else.

ESSENTIALIZE   is another rotten -ize word. Shudder at it.

ETHNIC   has become an overused noun loosely referring to foreign groups. It should be allowed to remain an adjective designating any of the basic divisions of mankind, as distinguished by customs, characteristics, languages, etc. An Italian in the United States is not an ethnic; he's a south European immigrant. Unfortunately, it seems to be catching on as a noun.

EUPHEMISMS   are words substituted for other words which might be too close to the truth or too offensive for some readers or hearers. Some cynics of the 60s and 70s called euphemisms "the language of deceit." Examples: *to rif* (reduce in force, fire), *search and clear* missions (for search and destroy), *protective retaliation* (for massive bombing raids), *terminated with extreme prejudice* (for execute), *underachiever* (for failing student), *surreptitious entry* (for breaking and entering).

EVER (EVERY) SO OFTEN   are not interchangeable. Each has its special function. *Ever so often* means "frequently and repeatedly," as in "He comes to visit ever so often." *Every so often* means "occasionally" or "once in awhile," as in "Every so often I go to see my family."

EXACERBATE   is an "in-word," pretentiously overused. Make it an out-word.

EXCESS   is a noun and, occasionally, an adjective. Those who turn it into a verb do violence to the language, as in "We *excess* our previous budget." Make it *exceed. "In excess of" is a grandiose way of saying "more than."*

34

EXFILTRATION   is a logical neologism. If *infiltration,* why not *exfiltration,* even though the standard dictionaries (except the MW3, which defines it as a synonym of *leak*) will have none of it? The OED calls it a rare word meaning the process of filtering out. The DOD definition is "the removal of personnel or units from areas uder enemy control." Like *retrograde action* it seems to be a euphemism for *withdraw* or *retreat.*

EXIT   cannot take an object. You *exit from* a room; you don't *exit* the room.

EXPEDITE   is a word in good standing that gets used too much because it sounds more important than *speed up, hasten,* or *do quickly.*

EXPERTISE   is a French noun meaning expertness or skill. Like *know-how* it is used *ad nauseam.* It sounds more sophisticated than *skill, expertness,* or *ability.* Cool it!

EXPONENTIAL   is a fashionable misuse of a mathematical term (referring to the small number above and to the right of a number to show how many times the number is to be multiplied by itself). Some people like to sound very knowledgeable by saying that something is *exponentially* greater than something else. Why not say it's much bigger, larger, etc.?

EXPONENTIATE   is gobbledygook, still unlisted even in MW3, from the algebraic definition of *exponent.* God only knows what it means.

EXPOUND   is an overused synonym for *explain.*

EXQUISITE   should be pronounced with the accent on "ex-", not on "quiz." Most men don't use such a dandified word. Many ladies think the secondary pronunciation ex-KWI-zit is more romantic than EX-kw' zit.

EXTERNALIZE.   Add it to *prioritize* and *conceptualize* as an undesirable.

EXTRACT   means to "pull out," as a dentist *extracts* teeth. Helicopters these days *extract* (and *insert*) troops. The etymology of the word, from the Latin *extrahere,* "to draw out," no doubt supports such a meaning, but it will seem odd to civilians, who understand that teeth, promises, juice, and quotations, but not people, can be extracted. As a noun the word means a concentrate or a passage from a book.

35

EYEBALL   is a noun, not a verb. As a synonym for "look at" or "see" it is deplorable. "Eyeball-to-eyeball" is a cliché, already beginning to fade. It evokes an uncomfortable image.

FACET.   See **area.**

FACTOR.   See **area.** The language would be better off if quotas could be imposed on the use of words like *factor, field, area, facet,* etc.

FALL OFF OF.   Knock off the *of.*

FALLOUT,   which orignally meant *radioactive fallout,* is now extended by the busy makers of clever images, which all too quickly become clichés, to mean "reaction" (to news events or controversial statements) and "by-product" (see **spin-off**). Leave it to the nuclear specialists.

FANTASTIC   has become a synonym for anything or anyone superb, handsome, delightful, as extravagantly used by teen-agers and other gushers. Its real meaning of "incredible" or "imaginary" has almost disappeared. Too bad!

FARTHER, FURTHER   are interchangeable, according to most dictionaries, but careful writers use *farther* to measure physical distance, saving *further* to measure degree or quantity, often in a figurative sense. "The farther away you get, the better," "Further than that, I have nothing more to say." 80% of the Harper panel thus distinguish between them.

FAR OUT,   meaning odd, unconventional, hard to understand, is slang.

FAT CITY   was orignally jazz musicians' slang for "unhip" (square) people. Later it meant the good life. Now it is the self-help word for unrealized potential.

FEBRUARY   should keep its correct "roo" syllable, which careless speakers, including far too many radio and television speakers, omit. MW3 accepts FEB-you-ery, faithful to its purpose of debasing English by accepting common, even though faulty usage as correct. By the same process *arctic* has begun to lose its "ark" syllable.

FEEDBACK   is a term used in electronics which has been taken over as a smart metaphor meaning "reaction" or "response." It grows tiresome.

FEWER   See **less.**
Wrong: He has less officers under him than I have.
Right: He has fewer officers under him than I have.
Right: A general has less to do than a colonel. A woman has less strength than a man.
85% of the Harper panel observe the distinction in writing.

FINALIZE.   Jargon. Say "end," "complete," or "conclude."

FIRESTORM   is a military term, taken over during the Watergate affair to describe, figuratively, the public reaction by mail, telegrams, etc. to the revelations of deceit and dishonesty. DOD defines it as "a stationary mass fire, generally in built-up urban areas, generating strong, inrushing winds from all sides; the winds keep the fire from spreading, while adding fresh oxygen to increase their intensity." The cause of the *firestorm,* of course, is intensive bombing.

FIRSTLY   is superfluous elegance for *first.*

FIRST TWO, TWO FIRST,   as in "The *two first (first two)* candidates will have a run-off election," are both acceptable, though 81% of the Harper panel prefer *first two.*

FISCAL   is a good word. Don't pronounce it "physical" or vice versa.

FLAIR, FLARE   are not interchangeable, though some dictionaries try to make them so. A *flair* is a natural interest or ability; *flare* (which may also be a verb) is an outburst of flame or a sudden, brief outburst of emotion.

FLAMMABLE, INFLAMMABLE   are exact synonyms. *Inflammable,* the older and preferable term, does *not* mean "not flammable," through fussy insurance underwriters are afraid that people who think the prefix "in" always means "not" might misunderstand the label "Inflammable" on tank cars. 73% of the Harper panel do not use the word *flammable.*

FLAP,   originally Army slang meaning a state of panicky confusion, has now come to mean any minor crisis or problem. Though MW 3 accepts it as standard, Random House still calls it slang. It's an addictive word. See **unflappable.**

FLAT-HAT, TO   is a brilliant contemporary coinage meaning "to fly low," "hedgehop" in a plane. It can also mean "to show off." The word is based on an alleged incident in which a by-stander's hat was crushed by the undercarriage of a plane flying dangerously low.

37

FLOUT, FLAUNT   are a very slippery pair, frequently confused. Misuse deserves and often gets ridicule. When you *flaunt,* you make an ostentations display as of virtue or a well-shaped leg; when you *flout,* you express contempt for and reject something. 97% of the Harper panel believe that the distinction between the words must be preserved. The *Harper Dictionary* says, "It is doubtful if any two words are more frequently misused, each for the other, than *flaunt* and *flout.*" Stop *flaunting* when you mean *flouting.*

FLOWCHARTING   is a gobbledygook verb formed from a noun. Does it mean anything to anybody but a computer specialist?

FLUSTRATE   is an error for *frustrate,* to which good ole boys are partial.

FOOT,FEET.   A man is a *six-footer;* he is six *feet* tall. It's a ten-*foot* barge pole, not a ten-*feet* one, but it is a pole ten *feet* long. In phrases before a noun (e.g., 12-*foot* jump, seven-*foot* center), use the singular; after a noun or pronoun it's correctly a plural (e.g., "He's six feet three inches tall").

FORCIBLE, FORCEFUL   are another slippery pair. *Forcible* means done with force, as a *forcible* entry; *forceful* means vigorous, effective, powerful. The distinction is fine, and some dictionaries say the two words can be used interchangeably. Don't.

FOREMOST,   thought by some to be an uncomparable adjective, like *unique* and *essential,* should refer to only one person or thing. Most of us, including 72% of the Harper panel, let it apply to more than two: "He is among the foremost professors of history in the country."

FOR FREE   was no doubt at first a humorous confusion of "for nothing" and "free." Though it is redundant and rather silly—and has no grammatical justification—it is recorded as acceptable by MW3, not by other dictionaries.

FORMALLY, FORMERLY   are a slippery pair, not close enough in meaning so that a normally bright person will misuse them.

FORMIDABLE   should be pronounced with the accent on the first syllable, as any good dictionary but the permissive MW3 will tell you. It alone allows the accent to fall on *mid,* a concession to ignorant usage.

FORTE,   meaning a special ability or interest, is pronounced fort, not fortay. *Forte,* pronounced fortay, means loud (in music).

FORTHCOMING. O.K. when it means "about to appear," "approaching," "available." It does not mean "candid" or "zealous," though it has such a meaning on many a fitness report. Only the MW3 among contemporary dictionaries allows the meaning of "affable," "sociable," "approachable."

FRACTIONATE is a word used by chemists, meaning to separate a mixture into its parts by crystallization, distillation, etc. Lovers of gobbledygook have appropriated it to apply to society, problems, etc. Prefer simple to pretentious words.

FRAGGING is military slang for any violent action against overly hard-nosed superiors.

FRAME OF REFERENCE is one of those orotund phrases favored by pompous speakers. It doesn't really have to mean anything.

FRANKENSTEIN is the name of the doctor who created a monster, in Mary Shelley's novel of that name, not the name of the monster. Don't confuse them. Say "Frankenstein's monster," if you can't think of a more original phrase.

FRIENDLY is an adjective meaning "not hostile." During the Vietnam War it became a noun meaning "not an enemy." American Heritage admits only the plural, *friendlies,* as a noun. Random House doesn't like it as a noun. Neither does the OED. But count on the Merriam Third (and Second, in this case) to support usage. What's the matter with *friend or ally?*

FROM WHENCE is a redundancy, in spite of the Bible. *Whence* is enough.

FULL is considered by some to be another uncomparable adjective, arguing that when a bottle is *full,* it can't be *more full* or *fuller* than another *full* bottle. We've extended the word, however, to mean "well stocked," as a "cellar full of wine," and of course we can say that one cellar is *fuller* than another. Don't get too pedantic.

FULSOME means offensive to good taste, usually because of excess or insincerity. *"Fulsome* praise" is *not* honest commendation.

FUN is a noun, not an adjective. Leave *"fun* party" and *"fun* time" to uninformed juveniles and gushing females.

FUNGIBLE   is a legal term referring to something that can be used in place of something else. Anyone who uses it instead of "substitute" will display his knowledge of Latin or the law, but almost nobody will know what he is talking about.

GANTLET, GAUNTLET   have both come to mean vaguely the same thing, "ordeal," though their real meanings are far apart. A *gauntlet* (French for "little glove") is a glove, thrown before an enemy by a challenger to a duel. A *gantlet* (Swedish for "running course") is a double line of warriors, guards, etc., armed with clubs, between which a person being punished must run. Most dictionaries now allow both words to have the sense of "challenge." Remember that *gauntlet* is the better word for "challenge," and let your victim "run the *gantlet.*"

GAMBIT   is a chess term meaning a maneuver or action to gain an advantage. If you confuse it with *gamut,* a musical term meaning whole range or scale, don't risk embarrassment by using it at all.

GAMUT   See **gambit** and **spectrum.**

GASID (INDIGESTION)   is a repellent blend of gas and acid. Boycott the users!

GAY   used to be a happy word. It has been pre-empted by the homosexuals, another beautiful old word made useless except in a sense it has only recently acquired.

GENT   is a vulgar abbreviation of *gentlemen.* It may be acceptable on the door of a restroom in a third-rate restaurant, but not in an address to a male audience.

GENUINE   should be pronounced JEN-you-in, not JEN-yoo-ine.

GERONIMO,   slang for liquor spiked with barbiturates.

GHETTONOMICS   is a smartass hybrid combining an Italian root with a Greek suffix. The effect is just too damned clever.

GIFT   is a noun, though it is sometimes used as a verb. Let the English *gift* scholarships, awards, Christmas presents, and the like. Americans should normally keep it a noun (except as a participle, *gifted,* meaning "talented"). 95% of the Harper panel use it exclusively as a noun.

GLAD FOR HAPPY   is a drafting officer's lament when his boss makes what he thinks are trivial changes in his compositions. Don't be too sure, however, that synonyms are inevitably interchangeable.

GLITCH   is slang for a surge of energy that causes malfunction of a machine, hence a synonym for **gremlin.**

GLOBAL   becomes grandiose when overused for "world-wide" (as does *globe* for *world).*

GOBBLEDYGOOK   is any spoken or written word or phrase that is pompous, wordy, involved, or heavily Latinized. Variations of it are *bureaucratese, Pentagonese, computerese,* and *educationese.* Samples: "manpower mix determination," "to obviate the cyclical lack," "life cycle costing methodology," "source selection evaluation criteria," "prioritize," "decisioned," "oversight capability," "survivable retaliatory capability," "nondiscernible micro-binocular" (dart gun with silencer). Sometimes, though not usually, even the uninitiated can translate, guessing, for example, that "qualitative advancement" means "promotion on merit."

GONNA, GOTTA   are careless pronunciations of "going to" and "got to," subscribed to by most popular singers. *Gonna* is all but universal. The words are beginning to be written that way, even when they are not in ballads. Sad!

GOOD   used as an adverb is an illiteracy, especially when accompanied by another adjective abused as an adverb, "real": "He played real good last week." Edwin Newman has recorded some horrendous quotations, especially emanating from athletes and sports announcers, in *A Civil Tongue:* "He ran the curve good;" "Evelyn Ashford comes from behind very good;" "The fight turned out pretty good."

GOOK   is military slang for any Southeast Asian. It is "used disparagingly," according to MW 3. New World calls it "a vulgar, offensive term of hostility and contempt." As the final syllable of *gobbledygook* it means dirt or dung.

GO PUBLIC,   which used to apply only to corporate issue of stock for purchase by the general public, can now refer to any revelation to the public. It is an addictive phrase. "Say publicly" does the job without suggesting that the announcement is covering up something or being used defensively.

41

GOT meaning "must" may have MW 3 sanction, but it's an ugly sound that can easily be avoided by "must" or "have to." *Gotta go* is a common ailment among careless speakers. *Got married* is inelegant for "were married." *Got* and *gotten* are both acceptable past participles of *get.*

GOVERNMENT. Please keep the "n" sound and don't imitate President Ford's "gumment" or say GUV-uh-ment.

GRAB as in "how does that grab you?" is idiot talk, like "how's about it?"

GRADUATE (verb) is intransitive. You don't *graduate* a university, you *graduate from* a university.

GRAYHAIR (verb) is slang for getting help from an older person.

GREMLIN was a World War II invention, a mischievous, invisible creature who loved to cause mechanical difficulties, especially in airplanes. It has become a standard word, with slang synonyms, like *bug* and *glitch* (the latter a word used by electrical specialists to describe a malfunction in electronic equipment). *Gremlin* is the best word of the lot and will no doubt outlive the others.

GRIMACE may be pronounced gri-MAYSS (as its only allowed pronunciation was until the middle of this century) or GRIM-iss, as most people now say it.

GROSS, GROSS OUT are adolescent slang. *Gross out* is particularly obnoxious.

GUARANTEE should be pronounced ger (rhyming with hair) -n-tē, not gar (rhyming with far).

GUIDELINES. O.K., but let up on it.

GUT-ISSUE. An "in-word," disgustingly overused.

HACK IT, a slang phrase made immortal by President Nixon, along with the equally inelegant "tough it out," the first meaning "put up with," the second "brazen it out," will forever have a touch of sinister vulgarity.

HAIRY is slang for "difficult," "frightening," "dangerous," "unpleasant," all better words which suggest no silly connotations as *hairy* (covered with hair) does. Random House does not list this meaning; MW3, of course, does, without labeling it slang.

42

HANG-OUT ROAD   has an offensive association with the Watergate scandal. Mr. Nixon at that time decided not to take "the hang-out road," that is, to tell the truth. Barnhart lists "let it all *hang out* (as distinguished from *hangout)* as meaning "to be carefree and uninhibited; let one's hair down." The phrase now has a tinge of deceit that makes it objectionable even as slang.

HANGED, HUNG   are accepted as synonymous by most dictionaries. Careful writers and speakers, however, keep the original distinction of *hanged* for an execution by hanging, *hung,* for juries and slabs of meat. 55% of the Harper panel so prefer.

HANG-UP,   meaning "a problem, fixation, sense of irritation," listed with this meaning only by MW3, may survive beyond the slang stage, for it is a vivid phrase, currently overused.

HARASS   now seems to be almost universally pronounced "her ass", though the original pronunciation with stress on the first syllable is preferable and less anatomical. It comes from a French word meaning "to set a dog on."

HARD-NOSED   is slang for "aggressively stubborn." A *hard-nosed* supervisor is one determined to do his job and make others do theirs without concern for personal feelings or finese.

HARDLY   is a negative and should not be used with another negative as in "without hardly a protest, the meeting was adjourned" or "I can't hardly understand him." Say "with hardly" and "can hardly," or recast the sentences.

HARDWARE, SOFTWARE.   These are rather cute words, used by computer specialists to distinguish between the semi-human machines and the programming material on which they feed. The uninitiated find them vaguely irritating.

HASSLE   seems to be a fairly useful new slang word meaning a struggle or heated discussion. It tends to replace more vigorous words, however, and to become as addictive as "y'know" or "point in time," so that everything is a *hassle* or we are constantly being *hassled.* Use it sparingly if at all.

HAVE A HANDLE ON   is contemporary slang for "to get under control." It is on the vulgar side.

HE (SHE) IS A MAN (WOMAN) WHO. . .   is a redundancy. "He (she) is..." is enough.

43

HEALTHFUL, HEALTHY   are commonly interchanged, though they mean quite different things. *Healthful* means giving or promoting health; *healthy* means having good health. A climate is healthful, not healthy; only a person is healthy (except when the word means a considerable quantity, as in "a healthy serving of pie").

HEART-RENDING,   an obsolescent cliché, must not be confused with *heart-rendering,* which means turning the heart to lard. The latter is an ignorant word-substitution, like "I've just put in a *stench* at the Pentagon" *(stench* for *stint).*

HEIGHT   should *never* be spelled or pronounced *heighth.*

HEINOUS,   *if you must use it, is pronounced HAY-ness, not HY-ness* or *HEE-ness.*

HELICOPTER   is a noun, not a verb. Both the pronunciations, *HEL-*ih-kopter and *HEEL-*ih-kopter are acceptable, but not *HEE-*lee-uh-copter.

HIGHLIGHT   is beginning to be a flabby cliché.

HINDRANCE   is correct, never *hinderance.*

HISTORICAL, HISTORIAN   should be preceded by the article "a" not "an". Only words beginning with silent h should have the "an" article: honor, hour. The current tendency to say "an historian," "an hysterical woman," "an hysterectomy" is deplorable swank. You wouldn't say "an horse," would you?

HOMOGENOUS, HOMOGENEOUS   can easily trip you up because, though they are pronounced differently, they have similar meanings. *Homogeneous* is probably the one you want. It means "composed of similar or identical elements or parts, uniform." *Homogenous* is a biological word which means "having similarity in structure." MW3 says they can be synonymous. Other dictionaries disagree.

HOPEFULLY,   in the sense of "it is to be hoped that," though all but universally used and sure to become respectable, is almost always grammatically incorrect. "Hopefully, the sun will shine" literally declares an absurdity. If you want to be fashionable, say "hopefully" and additionally" as often as possible. If you want to be accurate, say "we hope" or "I hope" and "moreover." *The American Heritage* Dictionary's Usage Panel found the popular meaning acceptable to only 44% of its members. 76% of the Harper panel refuse to use it in their writing and only 42% in speech.

HOST   should be a noun, not a verb. 70% of the Harper Panel reject the verbal use, now approved by most dictionaries.

HOSTILE   is normally an adjective. As a noun it goes back to the 17th century, when it referred to *hostile* Indians. Since "enemy" means exactly what *hostile* as a noun does, why not use it? See **friendly.**

HOSTILE UNFRIENDLIES   is a double negative for enemy.

HOWEVER.   See **but.**

HOW'S ABOUT   is foolish jocularity. Think of it in its full ungrammatical form, "how is about," and you'll avoid it forever. *How's tricks?* is equally obnoxious.

HUBRIS   is a fancy word from the Greek, meaning "insolence" or "outrage." Those who like to show off their vocabularies use it ostentatiously as a synonym for "arrogant pride" or "presumptiousness." Use the simpler words.

HUMAN BEING   is the correct phrase. *Human* alone is disapproved by most careful writers.

HUMUNGUS   is a comic-strip invention (meaning "large") not likely to be approved by respectable dictionaries.

HURTLE   should not be pronounced or spelled *hurdle.*

HYPHENS   are useful marks of punctuation which many careless writers ignore, thereby often blurring precise meanings. A "five inch gun crew" might be considered rather below normal height. Make it "five-inch-gun crew." In "guided missile ships," is the missile or the ship guided? When two words together modify a third following word, use a hyphen: "well-earned rest," "a mile-long beach."

-IBLE -ABLE   suffixes cause endless woe for spellers. Look up *defensible, responsible, hospitable, formidable, illegible, permissible* until you feel sure of them. Then you'd better check again. They're bastards.

I.E., E.G.   are abbreviations from the Latin which require periods and are usually italicized and written in lower-case letters. *I.e.* stands for *id est,* "that is," *e.g.* for *exempli gratia,* "for example." Don't mix them up and don't use either of them too often.

ILLITERATE   literally means some one who can neither read nor write. It is widely used, however, even in this book of usage, to mean "ignorant" or "stupid." Only 32% of the Harper panel admit to using it in this broad sense in their writing, though 51% do in their speech. It's O.K.

IMAGINARY,   meaning something imagined, unreal, must not be confused with *imaginative,* having creative or productive talent. They are a slippery pair.

I MEAN,   like *you know (q.v.),* punctuates careless speech.

IMMINENT, EMINENT   are a slippery pair that constantly get careless writers in trouble. *Imminent* means "about to happen"; *eminent* means "well-known." Yet people continue to speak about being "in eminent danger." Don't.

IMPACT   is usually a noun meaning a more or less violent collision (though it has been taken over by sociologists, political scientists, etc. to mean "effect," "impression," "influence"). The military like it as a verb, but often use it incorrectly since it normally requires an object. "The shell impacted near me" should be "The shell impacted the earth near me." Why not just say "hit"? As an intransitive verb it is usually followed by "on," "upon," "against," etc.

IMPACTFUL   is jargon for "having an effect." It is a foolish use of a suffix by those who want to sound professional. Newman lists other misused suffixes and prefixes: *-ize, de-, dis-, -ive, re-, -fy,* loved by people in government and education to form impressive if not very clear or meaningful words.

IMPLEMENTATION   means "a plan or project put into effect," "a carrying out." It's a good though pretentious word grossly overused.

IN OR WITH REGARDS TO   is incorrect. *Regards* are what you send your friends. The correct usage is "in or with regard to."

INCIDENCE and INCIDENTS   are pronounced alike, but have quite different meanings. Only the mentally retarded confuse them.

INCREDIBLE, INCREDULOUS   are a slippery pair. *Incredible* means "unbelievable"; *incredulous* means "sceptical," "unbelieving." Don't foolishly confuse them.

INCURSION   is a literary way of saying "raid" or "invasion." Leave it to the novelists.

INELIGIBLE   may look a little like *illegible,* but only a careless or stupid person misuses them.

IN EXCESS OF.   This phrase is used in excess of the times it is effective. Try "more than" for a change.

INFER, IMPLY.   This pretty pair probably trips up more communicators than any other of the booby-trap words. The speaker or writer *implies;* the hearer or reader *infers.* It is never the other way around. I *infer* from what you imply. You do not *infer* to me. You can *infer* only from something someone else has said.

INFINITIVES, SPLIT.   See **split infinitives.**

INFINITIVE, SUBJECT OF THE   must be in the objective case. Don't get caught with your grammatical pants down in such sentences as "The best thing for you and I to do is tell the truth." *I* should be *me,* of course.

INFRASTRUCTURE   is a fat way of saying "foundation" or "underpinning." The word was not recognized by MW2. MW3, of course, which welcomes the latest gobbledybook, says it is in good standing. Random House limits its meaning to the military installations of NATO. The OED never heard of it. It is so overused that President Carter asked that it not appear in official documents.
  The DOD *Dictionary* adds to the haze by calling it "a term generally applicable for [to?] all fixed and permanent installations, fabrications, or facilities for the support and control of military forces." That's giving a new word too much to do. It's nice to know too that we have *bilateral infrastructure, common infrastructure,* and *national infrastructure,* whatever they are.

INGENIOUS, INGENUOUS   are a slippery pair, not even close in meaning. Look 'em up.

INGRESS, EGRESS   are fussy substitutes for "entering" and "leaving." As verbs they are horrendous.

IN-HOUSE   is a very stylish way of saying "internal." It is so up-to-date that no dictionaries mention it. You can really feel that you are up there with the big boys when you say, "We have an *in-house* problem." *Out-house* has for some reason not caught on as the reverse of *in-house.*

47

INITIALIZE   is another manifestation of the wicked -ize habit. *Initial* will do.

INITIALLY   is a splendid adverb meaning "at the beginning," "at first." Why do some writers love it so much that they tolerate no synonyms?

INOPERATIVE STATEMENT,   immortalized by President Nixon's press officer during the Watergate hearings, is gobbledygook for *lie.* It is quintessential gobbledygook: pretentious, sneaky, self-serving, almost but not quite plausible.

INPUT, OUTPUT.   Perfectly good words, especially to the computer people. Don't be so fascinated by them that you use them to mean "effort," "application," and "production."

INPUT, OUTPUT, THRUPUT,   a phrase made notorious by some Department of State genius in a job description, won an award as the outstanding gobbledygook of 1976. See *input* and *output. Thruput,* in both spelling and usage, reveals the depths to which the English language has sunk.

INQUIRY   can be pronounced in-KWAI-ri (preferred) or IN-kwir-ee.

INSERT   means to put something into, like a coin into a parking meter or a word in a sentence. Helicopter pilots these days *insert* troops (and *extract* them). Such a use seems overly formal. Why can't the helicopter simply *land* troops? *Insertions* (and *extractions)* can no doubt apply to people as well as things, but the words don't *sound* right. See **extract.**

INTEGREE   is a mysterious word, probably derived from "integrate" by the process which produces "payee" and "advisee." To Marines it means an instructor in a professional school brought in from departments outside the school or an expert in a special military field brought in to help solve a problem. It is in fact a non-word.

INTENSIVE TROOP INTERACTION   is gobbledygook for "a hard battle."

INTERACTION   is a legitimate word meaning "reciprocal action," used far too often, largely as gobbledygook to impress, as a synonym for "influence."

INTERFACE   is a noun meaning "a surface that lies between two parts of matter or space and forms their common boundary." The DOD *Dictionary* complicates it, but keeps it a noun meaning "a boundary or point common to two or more similar or dissimilar command and control systems, sub-systems, or other entities against which or at which necessary information flow takes place." It is never correct as a verb in its current gobbledygook meaning of "confront." Phrases like "interfacing reality" are ridiculous. The only accepted use of *interface* as a verb is by a tailor who sews an interfacing in a garment.

INTEROPERABILITY   is a military coinage. God knows what it means. Deep-six it!

INTERPERSONAL   is a member of the growing gobbledygook "inter-" family. Don't be tempted by its impressive sound to use it when *personal* says what you mean.

INVITEE   is rude gobbledygook for "guest," though MW3 (the only standard dictionary to list it) gives it the additional meaning of one invited as opposed to someone not invited. Leave it!

IRREGARDLESS   is, of course, an illiteracy. Only the benighted or the irrepressibly funny fellow uses it for *regardless.*

IS BECAUSE   is careless and ungrammatical in the sentence, "The reason is because he couldn't get there on time." The reason is *that...*

IS WHEN, IS WHERE   are awkward phrases at best and, in definitions, absurd. "A fault in tennis *is when* a served ball hits the net or lands outside the service court." Recast the sentence: "A fault in tennis is the failure of a served ball to land in the service court." "A platoon is when two or more squads are under a lieutenant" should be revised to "Two or more squads under a lieutenant make up a platoon."

ITS, IT'S   are not booby-traps. *Its,* like other possessive pronouns (his, hers, ours, yours, theirs), has no apostrophe. *It's* is always the contraction for "it is" or "it has."

IT'S ME   is quite acceptable these days, more so, perhaps, than "it's him" or "it's them." If the correct predicate nominative of a pronoun after the verb *to be* sounds schoolmarmish, use the objective case and be comfortable.

49

-IZE   fathers more monsters than Nessie: *strategize, potentialize, maximize, prioritize, actualize, optimize*. Often, however it has legitimate children: *criticize, baptize, rationalize, plagiarize, idolize, crystallize, unionize*. Don't try to be clever, inventing words like *hostilized, youthfulized, disincentivized*.

JAWBONE,   up to 1961, when MW3 was published, had its literal meaning, though somewhere along the line it became a verb and acquired the meaning of "to talk without action." MW3 records it only as slang for *credit* (evidently a military usage). In MW3's 1971 edition it is given the meaning popularized by President Nixon: an appeal by a chief of state to labor and business leaders for price and wage restraints. It is still slang except when it describes bones of the head.

JUDGMENT   is a strong word all by itself. It doesn't need justifiers like *value judgment* (though both Random House and MW3 list the phrase as "an estimate of worth, quality, goodness, etc."). There was no such distinction in MW2, which considered that *judgment* alone was enough. We also have *judgment call,* which in gobbledygook means "make a decision."

JUDGMENTAL DECISION.   Just *decision* will do. Don't clutter up communication with sonorous, abstract phrases.

JUNCTURE   is a noun meaning "a joining" or "connection" or "a point in time." As a verb it is an imbecility.

KAFKAESQUE   is a pretentious, overly used reference to Franz Kafka (1883-1924), whose writings are disturbingly clouded. Use it at your peril. Someone may ask you what it means.

KANAT,   "an underground aqueduct with breather tubes which project upward through the surface of the earth," according to the DOD *Dictionary,* has been dropped by MW3, but appears in the MW2 as an Indian word from the Arabic, meaning "the wall of a tent." God only knows how it got its military meaning. The OED spells it *canaut,* describing it as an Urdu word from Arabic *ganat,* "meaning the side wall of a tent; a canvas enclosure." It was first used with this meaning in 1625.

KIND OF, SORT OF   are common colloquialisms in American speech, meaning "rather" or "somewhat." Don't let them creep into your writing. When correctly used to indicate a category, as in "This kind of bird," "This sort of event," don't be tempted to throw in a superfluous a: "This kind of a bird." And when you classify plurals, say "These kinds of things," never "these kind" or "those kind." And don't slip into hillbilly speech: "I'm kindly [for kind of] glad to see you."

50

KISS   is an acronym for "Keep it simple, stupid." Though it is a basic instruction for computer programmers, they consistently ignore it. Let it be a reminder to all communicators.

KITSCH,   a German word meaning sentimental, superficial, pretentious popular art or writing, allows you to show off your vocabulary. *Trash* does equally well.

KNOT   is a unit of speed, not of distance. Those who know the sea sneer at landlubbers who speak of "knots per hour." Leave out "per hour." A *knot* is one nautical mile (1.15 land miles) per hour.

KNOWLEDGEABLE   is a good word for a well-informed person, but for heaven's sake stop overusing it. Like "accomplish," "outstanding," "rhetoric," "overview," and "parameter," it tends to become addictive.

LACUNA,   Latin word for ditch or hole, means "a gap or space from which something is missing or omitted." Since most people don't know the word, you are bound to earn admiration for your learning when you use it. Gobbledygook specialists love it.

LAID BACK   is current slang for "relaxed." Don't use it in writing.

LATIN PLURALS   *Thesis, analysis, basis, synopsis* have final -ēs in the plural. Don't get smart and assume that all plurals ending in -es are like them. *Processes, services, offices, bases* (plural of *base)* do not have stressed final syllable. See **basis.** See also **media, data.**

Latin words ending in -um have plurals ending in a: *stadium, stadia; memorandum, memoranda; stratum, strata; curriculum, curricula.* We now also accept -um words with -s plurals; *stadiums, memorandums.* See **data** and **media.**

Latin masculine nouns ending in -us have plurals ending in i: *alumnus, alumni; cactus, cacti; syllabus, syllabi.*

Latin feminine nouns ending in a have plurals in ae: *alumna, alumnae; vertebra, vertabrae; formula, formulae; antenna, antennae.*

But watch out for irregular plurals: *index, indices; apparatus, apparatus.*

The Latin plural i sound is pronounced *ai* not *ee;* the *ae* sound is pronounced *ee,* not *ai.*

LEAD   as a verb has a proper past tense spelled "led." The noun meaning a metal only coincidentally sounds the same as "led." Get the *lead* out of *lead.*

LEARN, TEACH   are confused only by those who have not learned much from those who teach them. You can't *learn* anybody anything.

LEND, LOAN.   Though *lend* is a verb and *loan* a noun, dictionaries now also accept *loan* as a verb, and the two words have become interchangeable (except that *lend,* of course, is never a noun).

LESS, FEWER   should not be used interchangeably, but often are. *Less* applies to quantities that can be measured ("less noise," "less money"), *fewer* to things that can be counted ("fewer responsibilities," "fewer calories," "fewer whales"). The Harper panel was firm on this distinction, 85% observing it in their writing, 76% in their speaking.

LET'S YOU AND I   is clearly ungrammatical. *Let's* stands for "let us." If you really need *you and I,* change the *I* to *me.*

LIABLE.   See **apt.**

LIAISE   is the misbegotten offspring of *liaison.* You only save two syllables when you say "liaise with" instead of "coordinate with." Don't. Only the Merriam Third recognizes it.

LIE, LAY   are all too often incorrectly used, partly because the past tense of *lie* is spelled exactly like the present tense of *lay.* The principal parts of both: lie, lay, lain; lay, laid, laid. *Lie* is intransitive, taking no object; *lay* is transitive and must take an object. Don't make the past tense of *lie laid,* just because you think *lain* is affected.

LIFE-STYLE   is an addictive phrase like "time frame" and "problem area." "Style" or "pattern" alone does the job.

LIGHTNING, LIGHTENING   are confused only by the unwary or uninformed (though some provincial speakers pronounce *lightning* as *lightening*). *Lightening is the present participle of the verb "to lighten"* ("*We are lightening* his class-load.")

LIKELY.   See **apt.**

LIKE   has become a kind of grammatical wart. It forms a horny growth in careless sentences, having no more meaning than *y'know.* As a conjunction it has crept into permissive dictionaries so that "tell it like it is" is accepted as eloquent. The phrase is in fact both a cliché and a faulty use of *like. Like* is a verb, a noun, a preposition, an adjective, and an adverb, but *not* a conjunction (in spite of the dictionaries). 87% of the Harper panel disapprove of *like* as a conjunction.

LIKE I SAY   is a particularly irritating locution which is both incorrect and intrusive. Some speakers sprinkle "like I say" almost as liberally as "y'know." See **like.**

LIMIT,   meaning "to confine within bounds" or "restrict," must not be confused with *delimit,* "to mark the boundaries of something."

LINGERIE,   in spite of MW3, should never be pronounced with a final syllable that rhymes with "way." Such a misbegotten effort to sound French has produced "roodge" for *rouge,* "chase lounge" for *chaise longue,* and "suit" for *suite.*

LINKAGE   is a current "in" cliché. It isn't wrong, just tiresome.

LOATH, LOATHE.   *Loath* is an adjective, meaning "unwilling", loathe is the verb from which *loath* is derived, meaning "despise." When I am *loath* to do something, I am reluctant to do it. When I *loathe* something, I hate it.

LOOSE, LOSE   are often confused. They mean quite different things. Keep 'em straight. *Lose* is usually the one you want, but you forget how to spell it. *Loose* is only infrequently a verb.

LOOSEN, UNLOOSEN,   like *ravel* and *unravel,* mean the same thing, though the un- prefix seems to make them opposites. You can't expect language development to be logical, can you? Compare *valuable* and *invaluable, flammable* and *inflammable.*

LOST POSITIVES   are supposedly clever truncations of words which have apparently negative forms so that strange positive forms like "couth," "ept," and "sheveled" turn up in cute writing. You can have fun with "sipid," "gruntled," "ane," "ertia," "consolate," "delible," none of which appear in dictionaries, but don't inflict them on readers.

LURP   is an acronym for "long-range reconnaissance patrol." LURPED-OUT is slang for total exhaustion.

MACHO   is a fashionable abbreviation for the Spanish word *machismo,* meaning masculinity. It is overused to apply to anything associated with virility, from muscles to sexual competence.

MAN   is used without concern for sex as an unnecessary interjection in colloquial speech, as in "Oh wow, man!"

-MAN   is offensive to women's liberation nuts, who think that *chairperson* is less sexist than *chairman*. They don't know that *man's* first meaning is "human being; person, whether male or female." The result of their imbecility is the substitution of ridiculous combinations to avoid possible suggestions that this is a man's world: *cowperson, personhole cover, freshperson.* Don't cater to such nonsense. See **Chairperson.**

MANPORTABLE,   if you must use it, should be two words. Since "portable" alone means the same thing, "something that can be carried," like a portable TV, you really don't need the refinement of "man." If it's too heavy for a man to carry, he'll know without being told that it's *truck portable* or *helicopter portable.* But maybe the distinction is too subtle for a layman to understand. *Man movable* also seems a bit obvious.

MARTIAL, MARITAL   may have something in common besides the same letters of the alphabet in slightly different order, but no one, especially a man of arms, should mix them up.

MASSAGE   once had the simple literal denotation of a rubbing or kneading of parts of the body to stimulate circulation. Now it wears a leer (as in "massage parlor") and has been taken over by the inventors of clever new usages, which quickly become clichés, to mean "consider," "explore," "work over," as "to massage an idea or a proposal." The image is repellent. *Stroke* is sometimes used as an even more objectionable synonym for *massage* in the sense of "work over."

MASTERS   meaning Master of Arts (Science) degree is a common illiteracy. "Master's degree" is acceptable, but the full phrase is preferable. If you are too lazy to write it all out, at least put in the apostrophe.

MATERIAL   is not an acceptable substitute for *materiel* or, if you're going to be precise, *matériel.* The number of supply corps officers who have never noticed that we use the French word, not its English translation, is legion.

MATRIX,   originally a womb, from the Latin word for breeding animal, now means anything in which or from which something originates or takes form, such as rock containing a fossil or a die or mold for casting or shaping. Too many people use it grandly and inaccurately as a "source" or "foundation."

MAXIMAX DECISION   is insider gobbledygook for (usually) a business decision which will either pay off splendidly or completely fail. *Cf.* "Shoot the works."

MAXIMIZE AND MINIMIZE   are -ize verbs that have made it to the dictionaries. It's too bad for the language, but we musn't stand in the way of progress. *Maximization* is the noun from this revolting process. See **minimize.**

MEANINGFUL   has become an empty word used by diplomats to describe conferences and discussions in which nothing has happened. 70% of the Harper panel reject it in writing, 63% in speech.

MEDAL OF HONOR   is correct, not *Congressional Medal of Honor.*

MEDIA   is a plural, not a singular noun. The correct singular is *medium. Cf. strata, data, criteria, phenomena.* We have surrendered on *agenda,* now generally accepted as a singular. Hold the line on *media.*

MEGA   is overused for any large number: megaton, megadeth.

METASTASIZE   is a medical term meaning to spread malignant or disease-producing organisms through blood vessels, lymph glands, etc. to other parts of the body. To say that an agency of government or some other inorganic entity *metastasizes* creates a vivid but rather overwhelming image. Better leave it to the pathologists.

METHODOLOGY   seems to some to sound more professional and impressive than *method.* Usually it isn't.

MIGHT OF, SHOULD OF   for "might have" and "should have" is juvenile carelessness in speech. In writing it's moronic. Say "might've" and "should've" if you must contract, but don't make the "-ve" sound like "of."

MIGHTY   in the sense of *very* is acceptable in colloquial speech, but not in writing ("That's a mighty good piece of pizza.")

MILITATE, MITIGATE   are a slippery pair. Don't confuse them: "This decision militates against our future preparedness"; it is *opposed to* our preparedness. "The judge *mitigates* his sentence"; he *lightens* the sentence.

MINIMIZE   is a flabby verb (though for some reason not as pernicious as *maximize).* As a noun, defined by the DOD *Dictionary* as "a condition wherein normal message and telephone traffic is drastically reduced in order that messages connected with an actual or simulated emergency shall not be delayed," it is a word only a field officer could love.

MISSILE   should be so spelled, not "missle," as we correctly pronounce it. The British prefer to have it rhyme with "this aisle." They also like fertile and hostile.

MISSILE ENVIRONMENT   is military gobbledygook. See **environment.**

MIX   is acceptable as a noun meaning "a mixing" or "a mixture," but sounds better when applied to cocktails than to aircraft, ordnance, or talents. The DOD *Dictionary* doesn't list it, though it does violate the verb form by defining *mixed* as "a spotting, or an observation, by a spotter or observer to indicate that the rounds fired resulted in an equal number of air and impact bursts."

MIXED METAPHORS   are incongruous comparisons, figures of speech that absurdly clash. Edwin Newman lists several contemporary beauties: "Reagan could use his victory in North Carolina as a springboard to rekindle his campaign." "Do we have any alternatives or are all our eggs in one basket if he picks up his marbles and goes home?. . .Are we not caught with our pants down out there?" "We are split right down to the grassroots." "It is necessary to lay the foundations for whatever difficult medicine the people will have to swallow." Harper lists a triple mixture: "I have been keeping my ear to the grindstone lately and I tell you that we have to do something to get a toehold in the public eye."

MODE   is educationese, usually unnecessary: "in a seminar *mode."* Leave out *mode.* It's like *area, factor, facet,* an excrescence.

MOSCOW   is preferably pronounced MAHS-*koh,* though MAHS-*kow* is heard more and more frequently and is acceptable.

MOST   is regarded as a colloquial (and rather juvenile) shortening of *almost* by most careful speakers, though some dictionaries sanction it. "Most everybody will be there" is a cute, girlish way of saying "Nearly (or almost) everybody will be there."

Ms.　before a woman's name is supposed to liberate her from man's tyranny because, like *Mr.,* it does not reveal marital status. Most people, including most sensible women, prefer the old forms, *Miss* and *Mrs.,* and shudder at the pronunciation Mizz, which sounds like a backwoods pronunciation of *Mrs.* We already have a good use for Ms. or MS., which means "manuscript."

MULTILATERALIZATION　is a particularly revolting -ize word, which we can do very well without.

MUST　is either a verb meaning "have to" or a noun meaning a new wine or a state of sexual frenzy in an elephant. It should be avoided in formal writing as a noun meaning "an essential": i.e., "Keeping your shoes shined is a must." MW3 says it's all right, but the careful speaker or writer, knowing that it is a verb, avoids it.

MYRIAD　is from a Greek word meaning ten thousand. It is now used as both a noun and adjective meaning any indefinitely large number. It's a respectable word but, like *outstanding,* overused and hyperbolic.

MYSELF　is a reflexive pronoun, correct in such sentences as "I will do it myself." But please stop using it instead of *me* in "The Colonel asked Bill and myself to attend the conference." Harper calls such use "spurious elegance" and suggests that it is the result of fear of grammatical error in the choice of *I* or *me. Me* is one of the six pronouns which have objective forms, frequently misused because Americans aren't used to having objects look different from subjects. We therefore get "between you and I" and "who were you out with last night?" Keep the objects of verbs and prepositions in the objective case and don't duck the issue by saying "myself" or "himself." 84% of the Harper panel voted against this phony use of *myself* in speech, 88% writing. See **Objective case.**

NAMELY　is a pompous and overused substitute for "that is to say," which can usually be deleted without loss.

NANO　is a learned borrowing from the Latin meaning "dwarf." Space-age fans use it to indicate anything very small. *Nano-nano* is science-fiction jargon.

NAUSEATED, NAUSEOUS　are commonly used interchangeably, though *nauseous* means something disgusting or sickening and *nauseated* means to feel nausea, become sick to one's stomach. "I feel nauseous" really means "I'm disgusting." 76% of the Harper panel would not say, "I feel nauseous" when they mean "I feel nauseated."

NEEDLESS TO SAY.   If it's needless, why say it? A silly cliché.

NEGATIVE: A pompous way of saying "no".

NEGATIVE, DOUBLE.   Avoid. "It don't make no nevermind nohow" is an extreme example, with four negatives, but "I don't hardly know what to make of it," with only two, shows some lack of education.

NEOLOGISMS   are inevitable—and desirable—as the language grows and as social, scientific, political, economic, and other changes require new words. Among the new ones in 1961, when MW3 appeared, were *drip-dry, astronaut, count-down, teen-ager.* Among current new ones are *palimony, petrodollar, gasohol, meltdown, good buddy.*

-NESS   often makes strong nouns soft, flabby, and abstract: *ferociousness* for *ferocity, maliciousness* for *malice, respectfulness* for *respect, courageousness* for *courage.*

NEW INNOVATION   is a foolish redundancy. *Innovation* means something new.

NICE   is an overworked word, which unimaginative communicators apply to anything from a dinner to a person. It would be *nice* if we could give it a rest except where it means "exact," as in "a *nice* distinction."

NITTY GRITTY   is a passé slang cliché, probably from black argot. It supplanted "brass tacks" and "basic fundamentals," *(q.v.)* to mean harsh truth or core of the matter.

NO DOUBT BUT THAT   is a double negative. You don't need the *but.*

NOUNS, ATTRIBUTIVE   are common in English, and correct, though sometimes awkward. They are nouns which have something like an adjectival function before another noun: "cellar door," "road sign," "floor covering," "sports spectacular," "mystery story." "Terror tale" would be better as "tale of terror"; "research director and "education superintendent" would sound more dignified as "director of research" and "superintendent of education." "Educational institution" is better than "education institution." Don't worry too much about it.

NOUNS INTO VERBS. Though many nouns can also be correctly and gracefully used in English, e.g., *house, grade, play,* the tendency to twist nouns into silly verbs, especially when standard words are available, has become all too prevalent: *host, gift, task, bequest, position, guest-star, contact, input, access, impact,* and a host of -ize words.

NO WAY is short for something like "There is no way it can be done." It developed during the early 60s as an emphatic way of saying "no." It is an inelegant, rather silly, and now tired phrase, already on the road out of fashion.

NUCLEAR is so spelled not "nucular." The misspelling often produces an ignorant mispronunciation, which even the tolerant Merriam Third calls "substandard speech."

NUTS AND BOLTS: now a tiresome phrase. It's as overused as its predecessor, "brass tacks."

OBJECTIVE CASE. In English only six words, all pronouns, have objective forms which differ from the subjective or nominative forms: *me, him, her, us, them, whom.* These six cause no end of trouble because for all other nouns and pronouns speakers and writers don't have to decide which is subject and which is object. The result is the incorrect "between you and I" or the illiterate "Me and Joe went to town." "It's me," grammatically incorrect because the verb "to be" does not take an object, has become acceptable even to most grammarians, though "it's him" and it's her" are still frowned upon. *Whom* probably is more abused than any of the other pronouns. See **who, whom.**

OBLIGOR is a legal term meaning one who binds himself to another by a contract. Leave it and its miserable converse, *obligee,* to the lawyers.

OFF OF is redundant. *Off* alone is enough.

OFTEN. Leave out the t-sound.

O.K. is O.K., though perhaps not in a very formal document.

ON ACCOUNT OF as a synonym for the conjunction *because* is either used in fun or in ignorance. Since the hearer isn't always sure which it is, you would be wise not to use it except informally as a preposition ("He lost his job on account of his drinking"). "I'm coming on account of I'm a real party guy" is unacceptable both in speech and in writing.

ONE OF THOSE THINGS THAT HAPPEN (HAPPENS). *Happen* is correct because the subject is *things,* not *one.* 74% of the Harper panel agree.

ONE OF THOSE WHO, as in "He is one of those who always watches the clock," is a booby trap. The verb *watches* refers to *those,* not *one.* The sentence should read "He is one of those who always watch the clock." Better still, get rid of the unnecessary words: "He always watches the clock."

ONE-ON-ONE is a stubborn cliché. "One-on-one environment"is an absurdity.

OOPS is an acronynm for "Occasionless Ordered Pre-emptive Strike," a war that begins accidentally rather than by design. It is Black Humor Gobbledygook.

OPTIMALIZATION is a contemporary monstrosity. Even MW3 doesn't list it, but yields to *optimalize,* which is no beauty either, as meaning to bring to a peak of efficiency, "by the use of precise analytical methods." We can only wish that the precise analysis would extend to the formation of words.

OPTIMIZE is another -ize word recognized, unfortunately, by the dictionaries. Eschew it!

ORCHESTRATE is a current political cliché, too loosely used to be a satisfactory synonym for "organize" or "arrange."

ORDER OF MAGNITUDE OF is a grandiose way of saying "about" or "approximately."

ORIENTATE. Try *orient,* the correct root verb. *Orientate* is a foolish and unnecessary back-formation from *orientation.*

OUTPUT. See **input.**

OUTREACH is a fancy, redundant way of saying *reach* (noun). Browning's line would not be improved if it read "A man's outreach should exceed his grasp."

OVER should not be used in the sense of "more than." It should be limited to a physical position: "over the mantel," not "It cost over ten dollars."

OVERSIGHT   means "a careless mistake or omission" or "a failure to do something." In its other meaning of "general supervision," applied to many Congressional committees, it sounds important, but could be ironically misinterpreted. Let's not let Congress take over a good synonym for "neglect." What's the matter with a *supervisory* or, if you must, *overview* committee instead of an *oversight* committee? An *oversight* committee might be expected to overlook or neglect its responsibility rather than supervise it.

OVERVIEW: meaning an over-all impression or survey has become a popular pomposity: A Congressional committee which has an *overview* of a subject seems to be more dignified than one charged with surveying or reviewing it. See **oversight**.

PAIR OF PANTS   takes a singular verb. When *pants (slacks, jeans, scissors)* are used without *pair,* they take plural verbs.

PALUDAL ENVIRONS   is gobbledygook for swamp.

PARAMETER   is a mathematical term meaning "a quantity or constant whose value varies with the circumstances of its application." By some linguistic magic, because the word sounds so good and gives the user an appearance of authority, it has come to mean "boundary" (probably by confusion with "perimeter"), "conditions," "significance." To be on the safe side, unless you're a mathematician, don't use it at all. If you really want to seem to cut the mustard, drop *parameterization* into a sentence.

PARLIMENTAIRE   is another borrowing from the French that appears in no standard English dictionary (except that of the DOD). It means "an agent employed by a commander of belligerent forces in the field to go in person, within the enemy lines, for the purpose of communication or negotiating openly and directly with the enemy commander." Current French dictionaries don't mention it.

PARTICULARLY.   Watch that second "r." Say par-TIK-yuh-ler-lee, not par-TIK-yuh-l'-lee.

PARTY   instead of *person* in polite speech is vulgar. In writing it is as revealing as "gent" and "irregardless." Leave it to phone operators and lawyers, or make it only a social gathering.

PATENT   as a verb and noun is pronounced păt'nt. As an adjective meaning "evident" it should be pronounced pay't'nt.

61

PEER   has been done to death by sociologists. It's a good word which used to apply mainly to juries. Now we seem to have no more equals, classmates, contemporaries, associates, or colleagues. We only have *peers*. *Peer group* is **educationese.**

PER DIEM,   pronounced only "per dyem" in MW2, in MW3 is listed as "per deeum" and only secondarily as "per dyem," ignoring the old standard rule about lengthening vowels in the pronunciation of Latin words in English *(alias, alibi, alumni)*. *Per diem,* however you pronounce it, means "per day." Never say, "The per diem allowance is $40 a day."

PERSECUTE, PROSECUTE   are a slippery pair. *Persecute* means to harass or annoy; *prosecute* means to follow or take to court one accused of a crime.

PERSECUTORIAL   is a verbal abomination made familiar during the Watergate hearings.

PERSONA   is psychological gobbledygook for "public personality." Don't show off by using it unless you're a psychologist.

PER SE,   by the rules of English pronunciation of Latin vowels, should be pur-SEE (as in *media, Venus, thesis*), but since most people don't study Latin any more, it has become pur-SAY, and the dictionaries approve both pronunciations.

PERSONNEL   is a dehumanizing term for "people." Let them be men and women occasionally.

PERSONNEL TURBULENCE   is military gobbledygook for "unrest or disturbance among the troops." It's a fancy euphemism for what may be an alarming situation. Use it sparingly, in the knowledge that most people these days distrust euphemisms.

PERSPECTIVE   is tiresomely overused, as in "Let's look at it from another perspective."

PERSUADE.   See **convince.**

PERUSE   is a bookish word. Say "read."

PHASE,   like *facet, factor, area,* is an addictive word, usually meaningless. See **area.**

PHASE IN, PHASE OUT   are addictive abstractions. Since Random House accepts them as standard, they must be all right (though MW2 and MW3 do not list them). Avoid them as bordering on gobbledygook.

PHONY   has become so common a noun and adjective that it should have outgrown its classification as slang.

PHRASEOLOGY,   for some reason, often loses its middle syllable, like *verbiage,* and is so mispronounced.

PINPOINT   is another cliché beginning to wear thin.

PLAY BY EAR   has become one of our most boring metaphors. Don't be a parrot.

PLAYWRIGHT   is correct, not "playwrite."

PLURALISM   is a philosophical term which people throw around loosely to show how good their vocabularies are. It is customary, for example, to say that America has a *pluralistic* society, meaning that there are a lot of different kinds of Americans. O.K., but why not say so?

PLUS, ALSO   are often misused. *Plus* should not begin a sentence, linking it to a previous sentence (neither, for that matter, should *also*). *Plus,* like *in addition to, as well as,* etc., does not affect the subject of the verb: "His height plus his strength makes [not make] him a good player."

PODIUM, LECTERN   are not synonyms. A *podium* is the platform on which a speaker of orchestra conductor stands; a *lectern* is the reading stand on which he puts his notes or music. You cannot stand behind the *podium,* only on it.

POINT IN TIME   is a wordy phrase made famous in Watergate testimony. Like *time-frame (q.v.)* it says no more than *time,* but sounds more impressive.

POLARIZATION   is a good technical word fashionably applied in recent years as a metaphor for the concentration of people or ideas in opposition. We now *polarize* public opinion instead of batteries. It has become a weary cliché.

POO,   meaning "Program zero, zero," is astronauts' jargon for clearing an on-board computer and feeding it new data. By extension, a politician going to POO comes back with a fresh program.

POSITION AND PRE-POSITION   are dubious verbs made from the noun *position*. *Pre-position* is especially deplorable because it usually loses its hyphen and becomes the word for a part of speech. Artillery users, however, can't get along without them. They feel that "locate" or "place" or "site" isn't sufficiently professional. Even MW3 does not sanction this usage. If you *must* use the noun preposition as a verb, at least have the courtesy to put a hyphen after *pre*. What's the matter with "place in advance"?

POSSESS   stiff-necked for *have*.

POSSESSIVES,   that is, words with apostrophes before or after a final s, are still standard usage. Only the writer who doesn't know any better says "ships course" for ship's course or "womens rights" for women's rights or "officers club" for officers' club. The possessive may not be quite so obvious in "money's worth" or "two weeks' leave," but the apostrophe which shows that a noun is not a plural subject or object must be used. Possessive pronouns do not have apostrophes: its, theirs, hers.

POSTURE,   like *environment,* is a great favorite of the gobbledygookers, as in "fleet communication posture," "viable electronics posture." Leave it to the physical-fitness people.

POWER-CURVE   is a resonant phrase that only the elite clearly understand. Speakers who want to be sure that audiences respect their dynamism mention it frequently, usually as "behind the power-curve."

PRACTICABLE,   which means "possible" or "feasible," should not be confused with *practical,* "sensible" (when applied to persons), "efficient" (when applied to things). A *practical* man may try to do an *impracticable* thing.

PRACTICUM   is an academic word describing the part of a university course devoted to practical work, as, for example, practice teaching for education majors. "Practical work" says it more clearly. Leave it to college administrators, some of whom still like Latin.

PRECEDENCE   *should* be pronounced *pre SE d'ens,* but constant mispronunciation over the years has given spurious respectability to *PRES e d'ns.* Now you can't tell the difference between it and *precedents.*

PRECLUDE   is a pompous synonym for *prevent,* like *provide* used to the point of nausea by military writers.

PREDOMINATELY is not an acceptable word. It is an error for *predominantly.*

PREMÌERE, DÉBUT are nouns, not verbs.

PREPOSITIONS may end sentences, in spite of schoolmarms: "This is the man I spoke about," "When you're in my neighborhood again, drop in."

PRESENTLY does not mean "now," though OED notes that may have been its original meaning. OED now labels the meaning "at the present time" archaic. It now means "in the near future" or "soon." 84% of the Harper panel support the exclusive meaning of "in a little while, not now."

PREVENTATIVE is correct, but why use it when *preventive,* one syllable shorter, says exactly the same thing?

PRIMA FACIE is another Latin phrase better left to the lawyers, to whom it means "adequate to establish a fact" in evidence. It literally means "at first sight" and should be pronounced *prima fa-shie-e,* though long misuse has established *fa-shi* as a secondary pronunciation. See **bona fide.**

PRINCIPAL, PRINCIPLE are constantly confused by careless users. *Principle* is always a noun; *principal* can be both a noun and an adjective. If you're looking for a fundamental truth, it's *principle;* if it's the head of a school, it's *principal. Principal* alone is the adjective indicating first in rank.

PRIORITIZE is a particularly ugly piece of -ize gobbledygook. Edwin Newman, in *A Civil Tongue,* denouncing -ize words like *inferiorize, prophesize,* and *strategize,* quotes an Iowa public bulletin asking "cooperating businesses to maximize the accuracy and validity of information supplied by keeping it as localized as possible. If they did, then the need for vocational training could be prioritized." Newman adds, "Social and behavioral scientists never look back. Ize front."

PRIOR TO. Once in a while say *before* instead.

PROBLEM AREA. Let's have an occasional *problem,* just a *problem,* not always a *problem area.* See **area.**

PROCESSES is pronounced pra (or pro)-ses's (unstressed final syllable), not processes. See **Latin Plurals.**

65

PROFILE, LOW AND HIGH. Very fashionable gobbledygook.

PROFORMA should be two words. It's another fancy Latin phrase which calls attention to the communicator's medium rather than to what he is trying to say. It means "for the sake of form" or "as a matter of form." Stick to English.

PROMOTIVE, like *supportive,* is an affected usage. Instead of *promoting* something, the gobbledygook lover is *promotive* of it. See **supportive.**

PROMULGATE. No military order is ever *issued* or *published.* It has to be *promulgated.* Prefer the simple to the complex word and give *promulgate* a rest.

PROPHESIZE is not a word, only *prophesy* with that old devil -ize added. The user is trying to say *prophecy.*

PROTECTIVE REACTION OR RETALIATION is gobbledygook in its purest form. That is, it doesn't say what it means, yet is impressive in sound and number of syllables to satisfy the gullible. It is a euphemism for *bombing raid.* See **Euphemisms.**

PROVIDE, meaning "to furnish," "make available," is often misused, as in "provide one an opportunity," instead of "provide one *with* an opportunity," and "provide your family good entertainment," instead of *"with* good entertainment." Don't leave out the essential idiomatic preposition. It's also used too much, even when it's correct.

PSYCHOMOTOR is psychological gobbledygook for "the motor effects of mental processes," which is gobbledygook for "physical reaction."

PURSUANT TO is an obsolete business-letter phrase, which the careful writer should avoid. Try instead "as we agreed" or "in accordance with."

PUT ON, PUT DOWN are popular slang phrases. When some one *puts you on,* he is kidding you. When he *puts you down,* he is deprecating you. *Put-on* and *put-down* are also frequently used nouns, not quite ready for formal use.

QUANTIFY is a pretentious word that tends to make communication pompous. Most of the time "measure" would be better. *Quantification* sounds better than "showing numbers," but it's an affectation.

QUANTITATE   is an ugly variation of *quantify,* which is popular gobbledygook for measuring or estimating the extent or quantity of something. *Quantitate* does not appear in Random House or New World, but is listed in both MW 2 and 3 and is therefore respectable, if not attractive.

QUANTUM.   Leave it to the physicists. When you mean "amount" or "quantity," say so. Deplore the cliché, *quantum jump.*

QUICK, QUICKLY,   like *slow, slowly,* are both correctly used as adverbs.

QUITE   is usually a feeble way of saying "very."

QUITE A FEW,   which sounds illogical, is a well-established idiom.

RANDOMIZE   is an -ize abortion, by which educators and other lovers of gobbledygook can turn good adjectives into rotten verbs. It has to do with the controlled distribution of tests, samplings, etc. to yield unbiased data. The sociologists who love such constructions have another adjective for *random, stochastic,* which impresses the damn fools who like long words. We can soon expect *stochasticize,* which hasn't yet appeared in dictionaries. Neither has *randomize,* except in MW 3.

RANG, RUNG   used to be equally acceptable as the past tense of *ring.* Now *rung* is considered colloquial. Keep *rung* for the past participle: "He rang the bell"; "he has rung the bell."

RAP,   meaning "to talk" or "take part in a group discussion," is current slang (actually going back to the 30s). It probably will not survive since, like *dig,* it collides with the standard word which has a widely different meaning.

RAPPORT   is a noun which nicely shows off your French. Turning it into a verb betrays your ignorance.

RE,   which should be pronounced rē, not ray, is the ablative case of the Latin word for thing, *res.* The legal phrase "in re," meaning "in the case of" is old hat. *Re,* meaning "about" in letters is rude.

READ   is of course a verb, not a noun. In recent years, however, probably in snobbish imitation of a precious British usage, it sometimes becomes a noun: "This novel is a splendid *read.*" Tolerate it, but don't use it.

REAL   is not an adverb but an adjective and cannot be used as a synonym for *very*, except in substandard speech. "Real fine" and "real good" are high-school dropout phrases. See **good.**

REASON. . .IS BECAUSE   is always wrong. The correct usage is "The reason for his depression is *that* he has lost his job." If you must use *because,* leave out *reason:* "He is depressed because he has lost his job."

RECLAMA,   meaning "a request to duly constituted authority to reconsider its decision or its proposed action" (DOD *Dictionary),* is an exclusively military word. It was dropped from the Third Edition of the Merriam Webster, but appears in the Second as a colloquial Spanish word, used in the Philippines, meaning "complaint." American officers stationed in the Philippines before its independence must have picked up this useful word, now still heard frequently in the Pentagon. To turn a fine noun into a bad verb, *reclamor,* meaning "to complain or protest," however, is unforgivable.

RECOGNIZATION   shows the outrageous influence of -ize formations which can produce this foolish substitute for "recognition."

RECON   is the abbreviation for *reconnaissance.* Don't inflict it on laymen who will be puzzled by a non-word.

REDUNDANCIES   are phrases containing unnecessary words, which in effect repeat each other. Examples are *mental telepathy, hollow tube, free gift, new innovation, revert back.*

REFER BACK   is redundant. Since the *re -* of *refer* means "back", *refer* is enough.

REFERENCE   is a noun, a Johnny-come-lately verb, usually to be avoided.

REFUGEED   is a ridiculous verb. *Refugee* is one of the more respectable -ee nouns.

REFUTAL, REFUSATION.   The first is an acceptable though unnecessary synonym for *refutation* or *refuting;* the second is no word at all.

REGARD.   See **in regards to.**

REGRESS   is a Latinized way of saying "go back." Don't confuse it with *digress* or *egress,* and don't use it as a euphemism for "retreat." In fact, don't use it at all. It is also a stuffed-shirt noun for "backward movement" or "retrogression."

REGRETFUL, REGRETTABLE   are often confused. *Regretful* means "causing regret." Only people can be *regretful; regrettable* applies to situations, events, incidents, etc.

REIGN, REIN   should not be confused, though ignorant young people who do not remember the days when horses were common are likely to write, "He held his troops under a tight reign."

RELATERAL TELL   is a sample of professional military gobbledygook which the laymen can't understand even when it is defined in the DOD *Dictionary's* most elegant prose: "the relay of information between facilities through the use of a third facility. This type of telling [*tell* as a noun is not defined] is appropriate between automated facilities in a degraded communications environment." *Relateral* is not a word in accepted usage. *Tell* is mentioned in the Merriam Third as an ancient mound or a dialectal word for "talk."

RELEVANT   is a cliché of the 60s which has almost returned to its normal meaning of "pertinent," "to the point." At one stage it was taken over by youths who dismissed as not *relevant* whatever did not suit their "life-styles." They sometimes spelled and pronounced it *revelant.*

RELOCATE   is gobbledygook for *move.* You can *relocate* a family washed out by a flood, but you should not *relocate* from one city to another.

REMEDIATION   is a legitimate word, listed in MW 2, meaning the act of remedying. It sounds like gobbledygook, and one wonders why *remedy* would not generally do in its place.

REPARABLE, REPAIRABLE   have the same meaning, but *repairable,* pronounced re-PAIR-ab'l, is usually literally something that can be *repaired,* like a television set. *Reparable,* pronounced REP-er-ab'l, is usually figurative: "*reparable* neglect," "*irreparable* damage." Don't assume that they are pronounced alike.

RESIDE.   Try *live* occasionally. It's less pompous.

RESPECTIVELY.   Not to be confused with *respectfully* in the phrase at the end of a communication, which should *always* be accompanied by *yours. Respectively* means each in the order given.

69

RESUME, RÉSUMÉ. When used as a noun without the accent marks *resume* may be confused with the verb, pronounced re-ZOOM. *Résumé*, pronounced ray-zhoo-MAY, is the correct noun, but the spelling without the accent marks (though it retains its French pronounciation) is gaining ground. It means a "summary of personal data."

RETROFIT is a technical word meaning to incorporate in an older plane modifications appearing in new models. Aviators love to use it, even among people who have no idea what it means. It is popular goobledygook for "renovation" (literally "fit back"). This one may survive, though it still hasn't appeared in standard dictionaries.

RETROGRADE means "moving backward," "retreating," or "retiring." The military like to use it with "movement" to demonstrate that no soldier ever retreats; he performs a *retrograde movement.* Though the DOD *Dictionary* admits that such a movement may be forced by the enemy as well as made voluntarily, "withdraw" or "retreat" would sound less like double-talk. See *euphemisms, protective reaction,* and *regress.*

REVEREND is an adjective, not a noun, and the pseudo-respectful use in "The reverend will now address you" is wrong. So is *Rev. Jones,* though *Rev. John Jones* is acceptable. Address a letter to a clergyman, "The Rev. John Jones." Only MW 3 admits *reverend* as a noun.

RHETORIC has almost lost its real meaning of "the art or science of using words effectively in speaking or writing," and has come to mean "artificial eloquence," "bombast," or "verbosity." It often describes the wordy pronouncements of politicians. What a pity to let a fine old word go down the drain because of careless use!

RIGIDIFY is sanctioned by usage since 1842. It's still a lousy word except to anatomists.

RIP OFF, without a hyphen, is a slang verb meaning "to steal" or "to cheat." With a hyphen *rip-off* is a noun meaning a burglary or a cheating. The phrase is now deeply embedded in the language and, like *hassle,* may become fully respectable.

RUBRICS are headings, titles, initial letters (originally printed in red, as *rubrica,* the Latin word for red earth, suggests). People who like to show off their knowledge now use it to mean concepts, categories, classes, techniques, customs, formulas, glosses, just about anything they please. It has a nice, learned sound and suggests profundity. The hell with it!

RUGGEDIZE is listed by both MW3 and Random House. Pity! We're all infected with the -ize virus.

SAFING according to the DOD *Dictionary* is "the changing from a state of readiness for initiation [of weapons and ammunition] to a safe condition." It seems a pity to change a noun into a verbal form when we already have the verb phrases "make safe" and "put on safety." But civilians don't understand that military phraseology must sound briskly professional.

SAME should not be used as a substitute for another pronoun, as in "He received an incorrectly addressed letter and returned *same* to the postoffice." It can mean "the identical" or "the equivalent," usually in legal documents.

SANGUINE, meaning hopeful, should not be confused with *sanguinary,* "bloody," though both come from the Latin word for blood. A person with a robust supply of the humor *sanguis* was regarded by 18th-century psychologists as likely to be an optimist, as opposed to one with too much black bile, who was melancholy.

SANITIZE is another bastard -ize word loved by bureaucrats. The DOD *Dictionary* defines it as to "revise a report or other document in such a fashion as to prevent identification of sources or of actual persons and places with which it is concerned or of the means by which it was acquired." Sometimes it goes beyond its derivation from "sanitary" and becomes a synonym for "launder." All dictionaries accept it, though the OED, tracing it back to 1836, calls it rare. Too bad it isn't!

SCAM is popular slang for any shady operation. It has not reached standard dictionaries, but newsmen and the FBI like it. MW1 lists it as a Scottish, North of England, or Irish dialetic word meaning stain or spot.

SCENARIO is a word borrowed from the arts to be used *ad nauseam* to describe any plan, situation, agenda that comes to the gobbledygooker's attention.

SCENE has come to have a slang meaning of "situation" or "place where the *action* is." "A bad *scene*" is an unpleasant situation; "to make the *scene*" means that you're not missing anything. Leave *scene* to its old meanings.

SCHMEER in the phrase "the whole schmeer" is a usually inappropriate borrowing from the Yiddish.

SEARCH AND CLEAR   is a military euphemism for "search and destroy."

SECOND-GUESS   is acceptable in standard dictionaries as a fancy way of saying *outguess* or *predict*. Ultra-smart talkers speak glibly of using hindsight in criticizing or advising someone as *second-guessing*. Avoid it in writing.

SELF-ACTUALIZATION   is one of the pompous, vague phrases loved by sociologists. It hasn't yet reached any dictionary, but undoubtedly will as a fussy synonym for *self-realization*, which is pretty vague too.

SELF-DESTRUCT   is space-age jargon, both as an adjective and a verb. Leave it to missile experts and TV actors.

SENSUOUS, SENSUAL   are incorrectly used interchangeably. *Sensuous* refers to the senses, including appreciation of the arts. *Sensual* usually has to do with sex. 82% of the Harper panel think the distinction is important, in spite of writers' efforts to make sex *sensuous* (nice and soft) rather than *sensual* (physical).

SEQUENCE   is a noun, not a verb, except in MW 3, which approves of foolishly making nouns into verbs. Say *follow*.

SHOOK   is not the past participle of *shake,* whose principal parts are *shake, shook, shaken.* "I'm all shook up" may once have been cute; it is now a dull cliché. See **drag.**

SHALL, WILL   have lost the old grammar-book distinction that for simply futurity you must use *shall* in the first person, singular and plural, and *will* for the other persons. The reverse was true in expressing determination. Nearly everybody today says *will* for all persons and all meanings. There was a nice sound about an occasional *shall,* correctly used, now almost entirely lost.

SHOP   was once an intransitive verb, which could not take an object. Radio commercials and the new dictionaries notwithstanding, you should not "shop Woodie's" or "shop the PX." You shop *at* Woodie's or *at* the PX.

SHORTFALL.   How did we ever describe a shortage or deficiency before some genius thought of reversing "fall short"? *Longfall* hasn't yet found favor.

SHOULD OF.   See **might of.**

SHOWER ACTIVITY is in line with the tendency to make concrete words abstract, as in *problem area, combat environment, supportive.* Let's just have *showers.*

SIBLING, like *peer,* is overused. Stick to *brother* or *sister.*

SIGHT, CITE, and SITE are confused only by the semiliterate. The artillerist who *sights* and *sites* his guns is doing two quite different things. He *cites* the manual for both. *Site* is a fine word, meaning "to put in position, as artillery," to use instead of the monstrous verb *position.*

SILHOUETTE. See **profile.**

SIMPLISTIC is elegant gobbledygook for *simple.* Don't think that its use puts you into an elite group.

SNAFU is a WW2 acronym for "situation normal: all fouled up." It has been replaced by FUBB, "fouled up beyond belief." Inappropriate for formal communication. Informally, implying a stronger word, it is very emphatic.

SNEAK is a regular verb whose principal parts are *sneak, sneaked, sneaked.* Don't be cute and make the past tense *snuck.* See **drag.**

SOFTWARE. See **hardware.**

SO LOW OF A PRICE is illiterate for "so low a price."

SOMATOPSYCHIC sounds important. What does it mean?

SOME KIND OF is a current cliché, no doubt with a short life, implying a vague compliment: "She's some kind of woman" means she's a great person. Say so.

SORTIE by derivation from the French *sortir,* "to go out," has always in the past meant a sudden attack by forces of a besieged place on the besieger. The military still accepts this meaning of *sally,* but now most often use it to mean an operational flight by one aircraft. The DOD *Dictionary* also turns it into a verb to mean "to depart from a port or anchorage." So do other dictionaries, but it's still better as a noun than a verb.

SPEAK TO A TOPIC. You can speak to an audience or a person, but you can't speak to a topic. See **address.**

SPECIAL. See **especial.**

SPECIES   is both singular and plural. Those who think *specie* is the singular of *species* demonstrate their deplorable ignorance. *Specie* means "coin."

SPECIFICITY   is a legitimate word, but it has the earmarks of gobbledygook.

SPECTATE,   meaning "to be a spectator," is an offense against the language.

SPECTRUM   is an overused metaphor. *Cf.* **gamut,** *the* **whole schmeer.**

SPIN-OFF (SPINOFF)   once had meaning only in the stock market. Since 1961 it has acquired a new, vigorous meaning of "a useful byproduct" as a spin-off from missile research. It is one of the imaginative metaphors in vogue since the beginning of our space program.

SPLIT INFINITIVES   aren't wrong, but they are often awkward and ugly. "To really know" is better than "really to know" or "to know really." But most splits, especially when two or more words separate the "to" and the verb, can and should be avoided: "to more or less carefully write" is the phrase of a writer with no ear for music.

SPRANG, SPRUNG   are both acceptable as the past tense of *spring,* though *sprang* if preferable.

SQUARE ONE, GOING BACK TO   has become a very tired cliché, like "go back to the drawing board," meaning very much the same thing.

STAND DOWN   is a sturdy military phrase meaning "to go off duty." It should be two words.

STERILIZE   means "to remove from material to be used in covert and clandestine operations, marks or devices which can identify it as emanating from the opposing nations or organization." (DOD *Dictionary)* It's an improvement over *sanitize* in that it is a legitimate word. Of course, it can also have something to do with zero population growth. Why don't we limit it to that meaning?

STOCHASTIC   is from a Greek word, meaning "to guess." Pretentious speakers or writers consider it a marvelous way of saying "conjectural." It isn't. Some use it as gobbledygook for getting a job done by trial and error. See **randomize.**

STONEWALL   is soiled Watergate slang. Mr. Nixon used it to mean "refuse to cooperate." Its meaning to the Watergate conspirators dishonored the nickname of General Thomas Jonathan Jackson, who in battle stood like a stone wall. The less admirable meaning comes from British parliamentary slang, in which the verb *stonewall* means "to filibuster." It is also British cricket slang, meaning to bat defensively and not try to score runs. Let's not recall a disgraceful period by using it.

STRATEGIZE   is another unnecessary, ugly -ize word. Don't be tempted to use it.

STROKE.   See **massage.**

STRUCTURE   is a fine noun, an overused and unattractive verb.

SUBJUNCTIVES   in English are going out of style, and you can say, "If I was in charge..." rather than "If I were in charge..." Don't lament the passing of the old forms, and don't try to preserve them in outmoded phrases like "be that as it may," "as it were," "come what may," "be it said." You might preserve conditional *were* ("If I were you") and *should* ("If he should come") because they *sound* better than "If I was you" and "If he would come," but don't worry about it.

SUBMARINERS   are sub-muh-REE-ners, not sub-MAR-i-ners.

SUBOPTIMIZATION   is a linguistic monstrosity. It probably meant something to its inventor, but it doesn't to anybody else.

SUBSEQUENT TO.   *After* is simpler.

SUBSET   is one of those mathematical words like *parameter* which sound impressive enough to be used in new, still unrecognized meanings. It is a noun, not a verb, meaning a set, as of data, that is part of a larger set. It cannot mean anything like "to put under." Even the mathematicians find it hard to understand.

SUBSUME   is a fancy word meaning "to include in a group" or "to classify" or to show that an idea or example is covered by a principle. Use it at your peril. It is not a proper substitute for *assume.*

SUITE   is pronounced sweet, not suit, in spite of the makers of cheap furniture.

SUPER, meaning "very good," "first rate," "excellent," is an informal use of the prefix *super-*. Leave it, along with *fabulous* and *fantastic*, to enthusiastic teen-agers.

SUPPORTIVE is a very fashionable adjective used by gobbledygook artists who love roundabout ways of saying things, particularly if they can throw in some fancy words. They cannot simply support an issue; they are *supportive* of it. Verbal garbage! See also **promotive.**

SUPPOSITIONED is a barbarous verb which, like *decisioned, enthuse,* and *liaise,* grew out of our bad habit of turning nouns into verbs. See **suspicion.**

SURVEIL is another verb-maker's bad dream. It is the deformed child of *surveillance.* When you need a verb expressing this idea, try *survey.*

SURVEY IN DEPTH is an addictive phrase. Use it sparingly.

SUSPICION is a legitimate noun, an illegitimate verb. Only a person who does not love his language would substitute *suspicion* for *suspect.* Even the MW3 calls it sub-standard.

SWUM is the correct past participle of *swim:* "He has swum across the lake." It is not the past tense, however, which is *swam.*

SYNERGY, SYNERGISTIC are sound technical words taken over by advertisers and other linguistic show-offs to mean "cooperation" or "working together." Leave it to the doctors, who know what it really means. Doesn't a phrase like "synergistic convergence" make you sick?

SYSTEMS ANALYSIS is a brisk invention of the computer age. It has what is probably a sound technical meaning, which those outside the circle only vaguely understand. The word *systems* has taken on a mystic significance, as in *systems method, systems programming,* which could beyond doubt be clarified by more simply stated phrases, but they wouldn't give the same esoteric impression.

TASK has enough to do as a noun. Don't strain it to become a verb, even though all the dictionaries say you can, and it has been in use as a verb since Shakespeare's day. Try *assign.*

TASTY, TASTEFUL   are a slippery pair. *Tasty* means flavorful; it is applied to something that tastes good. *Tasteful* means showing or having good taste in art, music, clothing, etc. Only MW 3, showing its tastefulness, considers them synonyms.

TAUT, TAUNT   should not, of course, be confused. One is an adjective meaning "tight"; the other is a noun or verb meaning "a scornful remark" or "to jeer at." To speak of a *taunt* ship is sheer imbecility.

TENTAGE   means tents collectively. So does *tents* alone. Don't add to abstractions.

TERMINATE   is a proper word for contracts and leases, but it is tiresome when used exclusively for "conclude" or "end," applied to military actions.

TERMINATE WITH EXTREME PREJUDICE   is a masterly piece of euphemistic gobbledygook meaning "to execute." See **Protective reaction** and **Retrograde.**

THANKFULLY,   like *hopefully,* applies only to persons, not to things. You should not say, "Thankfully, the day was fine, and the picnic was a success."

THANK YOU MUCH   is a gross substitute for "thank you very much." 89% of the Harper panel would not use it in their writing.

THAT, IN THE SENSE OF SO,   as in "I'm not that tired," is acceptable to most editors of dictionaries, but should not be used in formal writing.

THAT'S FOR SURE (CERTAIN, REAL)   is colloquial. *For* is supposed to intensify the statement, but only makes it sound silly. It's not as bad as "He's doing real good," but it's in the same neighborhood.

THEM   is an illiterate substitute for "these" or "those," as in "I seen them guys before." *And them* meaning "others," as in "my brother, his friend, *and them* are coming" is provincial.

THRUST   is another current "in" word which once had force. Overuse has made it flabby.

THUSLY   is a vile word. Don't use it.

77

TIGHT, TIGHTLY, like *slow, slowly,* are both correct as adverbs. "Hold me tight" is just as vivid as "Hold me tightly."

TILL, UNTIL are interchangeable. Don't write *till* as *'till.*

TIME FRAME, like *problem area,* is an addictive phrase. To some addicts the word *time* seems naked without *frame.* Try it a few times without *frame.* The withdrawal symptoms are not painful.

TO INCLUDE is an awkward way of saying "including."

TOO, IN SENSE OF VERY is illogical, but acceptable in sentences like, "He's not too bright" "I'm not doing too well," according to most dictionaries. Avoid it in formal writing.

TOTAL as a verb ("Joe totaled his car on I-95") is still slang. It will probably sneak into acceptable usage, but hasn't yet done so.

TOUGH IT OUT. See **hack it.**

TRAFFICABILITY is another mischievous invention of those who lightly use suffixes to turn words into other parts of speech. The suffix -able normally makes adjectives of verbs. Here a noun, *traffic,* is warped into a new form which may be utilitarian, but is linguistically hideous. It means "capability to bear traffic." Prefer the definition to the word. Unfortunately, the usage goes back to the 17th century, and most dictionaries approve it.

TRANSITION is a noun, not a verb. Even MW3 doesn't approve of "The Colonel transitioned the procedure."

TRANSPIRE means "to breathe through" and, by extension, "to leak out" or "become known." To some, who prefer Latin to Anglo-Saxon words, it means "happen." It is not only a dubious but a damned pompous choice.

TRIALABILITY is gobbledygook which even MW3 ignores.

TROOP, TROOPS have an odd usage. *Troop* in the singular means a group of people, usually a military *troop.* In the plural it doesn't mean collections of groups, but simply the individual soldiers, "a thousand troops" are 1000 men.

TYPE is a noun, not an adjective. You are sloppily colloquial when you say, "He is a good type soldier" or "This is a Navy type airplane." Put an *of* after *type.* If you are addicted to it, at least put a hyphen between "Navy" and "type" in the sentence about the airplane. Even "good-type," however, won't rescue the first example.

UNBEKNOWNST   is a pompous form of *unbeknown.*

UNDEFINITIZED.   Only God and the creator of this linguistic abortion know what it means.

UNDERWAY REPLENISHMENT   is the grand, mouth-filling Navy term for refueling or supplying a ship at sea. The basic rule for gobbledygook is, whenever possible, to use polysyllables.

UNDERWHELM,   as the opposite of *overwhelm,* is not yet in acceptable good use except as a joke.

UNDOUBTABLY   is not an acceptable substitute for *undoubtedly.*

UNFLAPPABLE,   still listed in dictionaries as a slang or informal synonym of "calm," "unexcitable," may prove to have good endurance. See **flap.**

UNIQUE   needs no qualification. Nothing is "rather unique" or "very unique" or "more unique." It is *unique,* period.

UNSURVIVABLE ENVIRONMENT   is a particularly offensive sample of military jargon. The constantly abused word "environment" is here giving the ability (or capability, as the military prefer) to die. See **environment.**

UP   is frequently used in phrases which don't need it: "make *up* the dessert," "clean *up* the basement," "wash *up* the dishes." They are O.K. in casual conversations, but not O.K. in formal writing.

UPTIGHT   meaning "tense," is widely used. Random House does not record it, though MW3 does. Many of the Harper panel think its a useful new word, but 80% do not use it in their writing. 43% use it in casual conversation and 60% think it's an acceptable word.

UTILIZE   is a fine word, but occasionally try "use" instead. Nothing is stuffier than an official paper full of repetitions of "possess," "commence," "reside," and "utilize" for "have," "begin," "live," and "use."

VALUE JUDGMENT.   We don't have simple judgments any more. They are, thanks to our complacent polluters of language, always *value judgments.* See **time frame** and **problem area.**

VECTOR   is one of those technical words that laymen never understand. It is a noun with precise meanings in astronomy, biology, and mathematics. The fly-boys have taken it over to mean "a heading issued to an aircraft to provide navigational guidance by radar." Well, O.K., but don't make it a verb, and don't use it at all with the uninitiated.

VEHICLE   is properly pronounced without the h sound: VEE-ik'l, not vee-HIK'L, in spite of MW 3, which allows both.

VERBIAGE   like *phraseology*, has a middle syllable, which must be pronounced. And don't, for the love of Pete, spell it *verbage*.

VERTICAL ANALYSIS.   This piece of gobbledygook probably has a serious meaning. To a literal mind it suggests a session with a psychiatrist in which the patient is standing rather than lying down (horizontal analysis). That interpretation is probably wrong.

VERTICAL ENVELOPMENT   is a tactic of air combat. To a layman the phrase sounds illogical. How do you envelope *vertically?*

VIABLE   is a fine word, used in moderation. Since it means "able to live," its application to inanimate objects is absurd.

VICE   in the Marine sense of "instead of" is correctly pronounced VI-see. No one, however, will ever persuade Marines that it is anything but vīs, as in "Vice-president." Why we need a Latin word to say "in place of" is a mystery.

VOGUE WORDS AND PHRASES,   according to Harper, "are words or expressions that suddenly and inexplicably crop up repeatedly in speeches of bureaucrats, comments of columnists—particularly those of the political type—and in hundreds of radio and television broadcasts. These instant contemporary clichés soon become debased by overuse and lose their initial sparkle and freshness." Examples: *charisma, thrust, zap, rap, expertise, restructure, erode, input, flap, watershed, bench mark, overview, infrastructure, fresh out, phase in and out, feedback, escalate, relevant, clout, interface, parameter, peer group, synergy.*

VULNERABLE   is a good word. Don't sloppily pronounce it "vunerable." See **congratulation.**

WANT IN (OUT, BY)   is colloquial, to be avoided except in regional dialects.

WATERSHED   is one of the bright metaphors for "a critical point" or "important boundary," which has been done to death by the imitators. See **crunch, clout, thrust.**

WHAT'S WITH   is informal for "what's the matter with." Don't cut this kind of corner.

WHENCE. See **from whence.**

WHERE IT'S AT is an indefensible violation of grammar. "Where it is" is enough.

WHETHER OR NOT is considered tautological by some, who drop *or not.* 56% of the Harper panel think *or not* is unnecessary in this construction.

WHO, WHOM are so frequently misused that some serious writers have suggested that *whom* should be abolished. Most grammarians now reluctantly permit *who* to be the object of a preposition when it is separated from the preposition, as in "Who were you out with last night?" In precise writing or speaking, however, the sentence should read, "Whom were you out with last night?"
　　Who is subject, *whom* object. Directly after a preposition *whom* comes naturally: "For *whom* the bell tolls," "To *whom* it may concern." After intervening words, however, the correct form evades many users: *"Whom* should I say called?" is wrong. *Whom* should be *who,* subject of "called." "I spoke to Jane, *whom* I always thought was a good friend" is wrong because *whom* should be *who,* subject of "was," not object of "thought." Don't be trapped into thinking that *whom* has more éclat than *who,* using it to show your social superiority, like phony broad "a," even when it's wrong.

WHOEVER, WHOMEVER cause the same uncertainty as *who, whom. Whoever* is subject, *whomever* object. *"Whoever* comes early will get a prize" is correct; "I'll give it to *whoever* you choose" is wrong. *Whoever* in the latter sentence should be *whomever,* the object of the verb "choose." Be careful when the *whomever* clause follows a preposition which may govern the whole clause, not the single word. "The property belongs to *whoever* pays the taxes" (not *whomever).* You must also be sure to use the subjective form when a clause introduced by *whoever* is the object of the verb: "I shall recommend for promotion *whoever* does the most work."

WHO'S is never right for *whose.* It can only mean "who is" or "who has."

-WISE. Forget it, if you can. It's to well-groomed speech what an Irish pennant is to a trim uniform. 94% of the Harper panel avoid it in their writing, 82% even in casual speech. If you get in the habit, you can end up with horrors like "verbalizationwise," "situationwise," and "facilitizationwise."

WOKEN   is a correct but rather rare past participle of the verb *wake*. *Wake, waked* or *woke, waked* or *woken* are the principal parts of *wake*. Since the tendency is to prefer regular verbs, leave *woken* to the British, and don't let *wokened* creep in.

WORKAHOLIC   is a barbarous hybrid whose users believe that anything goes in the invention of new words. Anglo-Saxon *work* cannot be mated with Arabic *alcohol* any more than a cow can be crossed with a monkey.

YAY BIG (SMALL)   is very informal. Don't let it get into serious writing.

YIDDICISMS   are often colorful additions to the language. *Chutzpah (q.v.)*, for example, is a lovely word. So are *schlemiel, schnook, schmaltz, schtick, kibitzer, schlock, kitsch.* Look them up.

YOU KNOW   substitutes for a grunt in inarticulate communication. It seems to be falling off a bit from its peak in the 60s and early 70s, when "y'knoq" punctuated most youthful and other slovenly speech. It is still all too common. See **I mean.**

ZILCH   is current American slang for "zero" or "nothing." It is not listed in standard dictionaries, though H. L. Mencken in the 1948 second supplement to *The American Language* quotes it from a glossary of radio terms as meaning "anyone whose name is not known." It is not an attractive addition to the language. "Thirty love" in tennis is better than "thirty to zilch."

ZIP   is another smartass synonym for "nothing." See **zilch.**

On Gobbledygook

S cience fiction writers have often tried to create suspense by picturing the invasion of our planet by hordes of weird creatures from other worlds. They are usually more intelligent than earthlings and have superior weapons, but by human standards they are unspeakably hideous. We are faced by an invasion far more real and destructive than imaginary Martians. It is directed by highly intelligent beings whose positions as executives, bureaucrats, teachers, scientists, military leaders, sociologists, and the like make them very influential. Their weapons are official reports, correspondence, authoritative articles, books, etc. The invaders are as frightening and repulsive as any little green men in flying saucers. They are the buzz-words or gobbledygook presently strangling all forms of communication.

Gobbledygook may be defined as pretentious, wordy, involved, sometimes unintelligible jargon. The word itself, still cautiously labeled "slang," was invented by an American Congressman, Maury Maverick (1895-1954), probably on the base of *gobble,* which comes from an old French word for mouth. *Gook,* now, mainly a contemptuous military term for an Asian, is what the linguistic experts call a phonesthemic word, one whose sound suggests the meaning, in this case unpleasant. *Gook* is related to *goo* and *muck.* In short, gobbledygook is sticky muck *(muck* is from an old Norse word for *dung)* issuing from the mouth.

Gobbledygook is not a recent invention. Writers have indulged in it, mainly to demonstrate their learning, in all periods. We even have a word to describe one form of gobbledygook, any artificial, high-flown style: *euphuism,* named from a character created by the 16th century romantic writer, John Lyly, famous for his mannerisms and affectations. Lyly believed, for example, that "it is...a greater show of pregnant wit than perfect wisdom, in a thing of sufficient excellency, to use superfluous eloquence."

By Argus Tresidder, reprinted with the permission of the Editor, from *Military Review,* April, 1974.

How apt a description of some modern writing and speaking: superfluous eloquence!

Styles change, of course. What we consider heavy, involved writing today was once admired. The authors of the King James version of the Old Testament occasionally produced passive, involved verses like "O thou enemy, destructions are come to a perpetual end, and thou hast destroyed cities; their memorial is perished with them." Samuel Johnson pontifically declared, "He examined lines and words with minute and punctilious observation, and retouched every part with indefatigable diligence." Ralph Waldo Emerson weighed in with "A true aspirant...never need look for allusions personal and laudatory in discourse." We would not accept any of these examples, though they are fairly clear, as good, simple writing. For all their inversions and Latinized wording, however, they do not illustrate the modern evil of gobbledygook, which all too often means the deliberate choice of confusing or vague or pompous words and phrases.

In recent years, the use of gobbledygook by writers and speakers has multiplied, for several reasons. First, since gobbledygook usually sounds impressive, many addicts adopt it to give themselves a specious air of authority. Second, since gobbledygook is vague in meaning, those who are not sure of the validity of their ideas or who want to be imprecise find it useful. Third, since academic disciplines and scientific, technical, diplomatic, and other categories of professional emphasis develop their own distinctive jargon, those who want to be recognized as up-to-the-mark specialists or to be identified with their peer-groups like to use the language peculiar to those groups. Fourth, the increase in all the media of communication spreads the infection of certain popular gobbledygook words and phrases.

Here are a few examples of current gobbledygook:

1. "We must maximize the fact of our incumbency." This statement by White House staffers during the Watergate controversy is almost as pernicious as the crimes they tried to conceal. Its meaning comes dimly though the feeble, ugly word *maximize* and the inflated *incumbency*.

> 2 .During the analysis phase, interactive processes that explore all possible data orchestrations, projective simulations utilizing a full range of feasible scenarios, programmed walk techniques and structional zoning will enable the development of quantitative parameters for a real world master plan for public transportation in Lower Manhattan. (New York City Planning Commission Report)

I doubt that the writer of this remarkable passage really knew what *data orchestrations, projective simulations,* and *quantitative parameters* mean. He was confident, however, that few readers would challenge such a statement and most, though uncomprehending, would applaud the evident authority of anyone who could toss off such magnificent phrases.

3 . Evaluation and Parameterization of Stability and Safety Performance Characteristic of Two and Three Wheeled Vehicular Toys, for Riding.

This is the title of a study, costing $23,000, for the Department of Health, Education, and Welfare. We can be both indignant at the cost and scornful of the language, which, in simple terms, means "Why children fall off bicycles."

4 . "The core area is suffering from disinvestment and needs to be looked at in the broad picture. If prompt actions are implemented within the suggested parameters, meaningful and relevant objectives may be finalized." (Consultant firm report on a municipality for the purpose of getting federal urban renewal funds)

This bit of pretentious windiness seems to mean that the central city is running down, but that it is still salvageable. *Disinvestment* and *finalized* are barbarisms. "Broad picture," "implementing actions," "suggested parameters," and "relevant objectives" are pathetic clichés.

5. Note the frequent appearance of what is probably the most popular word in contemporary jargon, *parameter*. It meets all the conditions of gobbledygook: it is rhythmic and sonorous; hardly anybody knows what it means; its real meaning is so evasive that the word sems to fit anywhere. *Parameter* is actually a mathematical term meaning "a quantity or constant whose value varies with the circumstances of its application." It does *not* mean "boundary," "conditions," or "significance," as glib speakers and writers variously use it.

6 . The proposed implementation of the project involves the alignment of disparate elements which have not singly or collectively yet been submitted to the corporate consideration of the personnel selected at the appropriate executive level.

This inflated sentence was quoted by Anthony Burgess, a British writer who loves his native tongue, as a sample of "pedantry which verges on gobbledygook. This kind of language," he continues, "lends itself to high-level lies and evasions, as also to such monstrous terms as 'anticipatory retaliation,' which means knocking the hell out of the enemy on the assumption that they'd do the same to you if you gave them the chance." (*New York Times Magazine,* September 9, 1973)

Let's now examine the differnt forms of gobbledygook: technical words, illegitimate words, muddy words and phrases, and overused words or jargonized clichés.

Technical Words

Between 1934, when the Second Edition of the Merriam-Webster Unabridged Dictionary was published, and 1961, when the Third Edition appeared, some 17,000 new words had come into use in the field of chemistry alone. Most of these words, like those in other sciences, were technical. They are useful only to chemists or electronic engineers or computer scientists or whatever specialized group has a need for them. Technical words are not in themselves gobbledygook. They become so only when specialists employ them away from their own turf because they want to impress or because they have forgotten that the basic principle of communication is clarity and they are too lazy or too impatient or too addicted to jargon to try to achieve it.

Technical language is necessary and good so long as it is used only with those who know what it means. Pilots speaking to pilots can talk about "vertical envelopment" or "vectoring" or "airframe configuration" without confusing or irritating their hearers. Sociologists can talk to their colleagues, with impunity, about "motivational deficiency due to deprivation" or "ethical disorientation" or "developing the infrastructure." The mysterious language of the computer world, full of "software" and "input" and "flowcharting" is just fine for those who live in that world. Educators can speak intelligently to educators about "cognitive domain" and "psychomotor responses." A Marine can speak to other Marines about "sub-theater, theater conventional, and theater nuclear levels of warfare."

When the technical words slip over into general communications, the speaker or writer *must* explain them, seek simple ways of saying them, or leave them out. Some readers and hearers are so humble that they blame their lack of understanding on their ignorance; others are annoyed by the presumption or pretentiousness of the user; a few say, "Gee Whiz! This guy is smart." Whatever the reaction, the communication is broken.

In short, there's nothing wrong with technical words; just limit your use of them to the right time and the right place.

Illegitimate Words

Gobbledygook artists are never more happy than when they can devise some new monstrosity of a word and use it often enough to give it currency. For example, *orientate,* derived from *orientation,* has burrowed into the language like a liver fluke and now has dictionary sanction. We already had a good word, *orient,* meaning the same thing. *Commentate* is the same sort of bastard word. *Liase, enthuse, destruct,* and *surveil,* are equally unattractive. The formula, for those who take pride in their gobbledygook, is to turn a noun like *position, impact, critique, structure, suspicion, interface,* or *attrition (atrit)* into a verb, or a verb into a noun, like *abort, mix,* and *insert.* The most fertile breeding ground for gobbledygook is the suffix *-ize.* With it you can form shocking hybrids from almost any part of speech: *randomize, contaminize, containerize, civilianize, suboptimize, prioritize, bureaucratize, initialize, sanitize, undefinitize, conceptualize.* The suffix *-wise* is also handy for those who are unconcerned about grace in language: *weatherwise, studentwise, bodywise, appliancewise, logisticalwise.*

I am not suggesting that imaginative creativity has no place in the development of English, that we should discourage bold neologisms. Lexicographers can hardly keep up with the many colorful and forceful additions to our vocabulary. Words like *spin-off, astronaut, smog, drip-dry, jalopy, two-way stretch, count-down, teen-ager* are new within our time. For the most part, they are combinations of familiar words to describe new conditions or new products. They are precise words, which scientific progress or new discoveries or changes in social, political, and economic affairs have made necessary. By the same process some gobbledygook becomes respectable; you can fine *maximize* and *orientate* and *quantify* and *enthuse* even in conservative dictionaries. The words *polarize* and *politicize,* both overused today, seem nevertheless to fill needs and should not be condemned with the -ize abortions (except when they become clichés by overuse).

What I am driving at is that when good solid words are available, you should not uglify your communication by violating usage or producing verbal deformities. Why *position* something when *place* or *locate* is available? Why say *in-house* when *internal* or *local* would do as well? When we let central cities deteriorate, must we *ghettoize* them?

Muddy Words and Phrases

Most gobbledygook is not in the form of technical or bastardized words. It is far more likely to be combinations of conventional words which fail to produce clear images or arbitrary phrases which sound good but carefully conceal meanings or disguise ignorance.

Here are several examples:

1 . Families who cling to ethnic traditions may encourage a participatory orientation toward death by their reliance upon patterns of personal interaction rather than institutionalized procedures.

This sentence has no particular words to which we can object. Even *institutionalized,* a jarring -ize word, is clear enough. But the phrases "Participatory orientation" and "patterns of personal interaction" dim the meaning. Even after several re-readings the ideas do not clearly emerge.

2 . This is in the affective domain and would require an "interest inventory" type evaluation.

Only those familiar with the professional jargon of "affective domain" and "interest inventory" would have even a foggy notion of what this sentence says. Such ponderous, elitist phrases should be kept (as their users would say) *in-house.* Incidentally, they might look up the proper use of the noun *type.*

3 . What is the doctrine and technical interface concepts for the TAO Center Operation in a joint environment?

This is almost pure gobbledygook, marred in addition by faulty agreement of the verb. I doubt that the writer himself knew the meaning of "technical interface concepts." He probably did know what he meant by "joint environment," but few of his readers will, and many will believe that he abuses the good noun "environment."

4 . The initial phase of Data Analysis involves the development or modification of special analytical methodologies. These can include trip hierarchy modeling, computerized flow simulations, and data-orientated network restructuring. Methodologies used by the Urban Centers study and other current efforts will be employed wherever possible to facility input-output compatibility.

Computer language is a strange and disturbing product of our time. What are "analytical methodologies"? Why should anyone who hoped to be understood invent such deformities as "hierarchy modeling," "computerized flow simulations," and "data-orientated network restructuring"? Don't tell me that he could not have found simpler words to express what he was trying to say! He was obviously keeping the mysteries of computer science secure from vulgar familiarity. He slipped when he turned the noun "facility" into a verb, an error even in a gobbledygooker's book, but he comes back bravely with the impenetrable "input-output compatibility."

Sometimes the muddy phrases are euphemisms or evasions, meant to blur unpleasant or damaging facts. Thus *napalm* may become *selective ordnance; retreat* or *withdrawal* may become *retrograde movement;* the phrase "protective reaction air strikes" covers *air attacks;* an unofficial execution becomes "terminated with extreme prejudice"; "crop-poisoning" may appear as "resources control." A market researcher may conceal an error as "a demographic skew." A child who cheats in school is "ethically disoriented." A bad child is a "severe norm violator." A person who is fired is "dehired," "outplaced," "selected out," or "made redundant." A lie may be called "an inoperative statement."

Words are muddy not only because they obscure meaning but because some of them are pretentious, replacing simple words which might not carry so much weight and evidence of the user's large vocabulary. *Use* is less impressive than *utilize, make* than *fabricate, laws* than *statutory provisions, before* than *prior to, have* than *possess, do* than *accomplish, prohibit* than *militate against, happen* than *transpire.*

Robert G. Weaver, a teacher of expository writing at the Army War College, published an article in *Army* (July, 1973) entitled "Meet General Bafflegab, Chief of Obfuscation." In it he tells how he was asked when he first arrived, to describe his course, stating its purpose. He wrote, "To help officers write effective English." The colonel who reviewed the paper stopped breathing when he came to that sentence. He looked incredulously at it and then at me. The he said patiently, "Can't you say that in a little more sophisticated way?" I tried a few times and finally settled for his version: "To prepare officers for high level command staff assignments by cultivating the skill of writing."

Analyzing the rephrased purpose, Weaver comments:

> It says in effect: We don't know what it is and don't care to define it, but it has to be resplendent; and when people see it they must know that this is the kind of thing a high-level person does, so let's not get it confused with the plain talk of any ordinary mortal.

Weaver gives another example of fuzzing up meaning that in the light of Watergate stands out as a horror of communication.

> A manager somewhere is hobbled by an obsolete machine. He can't replace it as long as it works. If he could get somebody to break it everyone would be better off. He could write a memo: "Bill, break that machine." The stark clarity of that message could come back to haunt him. His boss might say, "How dare you ask Bill to break a perfectly good machine!" So the manager says something like this: "All aspects of the problem having been carefully considered, it has been suggested that certain accounting benefits may accrue to this office if the widget gadget on level 1B were rendered inoperable." Now, if Bill breaks the machine and there are no repercussions, the manager can take credit for having ordered the breaking. If Bill's deed backfires, the manager can say, "I didn't tell him to break it. I just told him to render it inoperable. I thought he had sense enough to unplug it. It's hard to get competent help these days."

A word-watcher in the C.I.A. has listed the following elegant words commonly used in the correspondence of the clandestine services: *caveat, rationale, thrust, interface* (as a noun and a verb), *dichotomy, lacuna, forthcoming* (in the sense of candid), *profile* (high or low), *silhouette* (high or low), *options, life-styles, posture, rapport.* Most of these words, he comments, don't convey clear meaning, but they sound "distinguished and important."

We might add a few more wetback words which have illegally entered the English language and become undesirable citizens: *capitulationist, culturicide, decisioning, disincentive, doctrinarianism, empirically validated, ghettonomics, preemptive strike, somatopsychic, wholenatured organic will.*

A Congressional subcommittee making a special study of "The Federal Paperwork Jungle," has estimated that the annual cost of government writing—letters, reports, publications—is $8 billion. If one government record were burned every second, some statistician has figured out, it would take 2,000 years to burn all those now in filing cabinets. Much of this vast accumulation, say the critics of the system, is the unnecessary result of gobbledygook, which one of them has defined as "a disease to which bureaucrats are peculiarly susceptible and which is indicated by a swelling of the vocabulary and a dulling of the senses." The subcommittee figured that a billion five hundred million dollars of the $8 billion go for writing an annual billion letters. If letters were concise and made free of gobbledygook, the government could save from $100 million to $200 million a year.

If by some miracle all current jargon were eliminated from the language so that today all bureaucratic communication would be, in Somerset Maugham's words, "simple, lucid, and euphonious," new muddy phrases would have to be invented for tomorrow because many writers do not *want* to be simple and lucid. They don't mind euphony, if "good sound" is all it means. The more resonant the word, especially if it is a Latinized polysyllable, the better they like it. But simplicity might make others suggest that their knowledge is not profound or their discipline hollow or their impact on society unimpressive; and lucidity is a dangerous quality, making clear where responsibility and understanding lie. Unfortunately, many people don't wish to be pinned down by what they say. If they are imprecise, they can wriggle out of responsibility for ideas that turn out to be unacceptable or disadvantageous.

The great evil of gobbledygook is not only that it is ugly and irritating and indigestible, but that it allows the user to get away with vagueness and irresponsibility for what he says at the same time that it makes him sound highly professional and articulate. We can forgive him even if we don't understand him when he overuses technical language because we can assume that his subject is difficult or abstract and that he normally communicates only with other specilaists. We're sorry that he doesn't take the trouble to get through to us, but we must defer to the experts in a technological age. When he deliberately uses muddy phrases to obscure meaning or to evade responsibility or when he is trying to impress us with his wisdom and his familiarity with "in-words," we have reason to despise him. This kind of intention to confuse, lack of truth, and use of euphemisms and other inexact terms are more and more evident today.

Clichés

I am not speaking about tired phrases like "cute as a bug," "crooked as a dog's hind leg," "Little girls' room," "as honest as the day is long," and other manifestations of folk wisdom and unimaginative figures of speech. I'm thinking about the pompous repetition of words and phrases that may have been effective the first ten thousand times they were used, but which have worn out their forcefulness: *point in time, time frame, thrust, clout, problem area, consensus of opinion, spectrum, orchestration, climate of opinion, environment* (as in "aqueous environment" for water, "modern environment" for today), *nitty-gritty, core area, combat integrity, phase, factor,* etc.

Before the time of instant national and international communication, fad words stayed around longer than they do today. Before it died, a cliche slowly moved from the big cities into the hinterland, and the small town enjoyed popular phrases, which had just arrived, long after they were shunned by the speakers in the cities where they were born. Today radio and television wear out words as they do jokes and dramatic situations by overexposure. "Nuts and bolts" and "nitty-gritty" have begun to nauseate, like "tell it like it is" and "can of worms." During the Vietnam war (which the cliché-makers decided to call a *conflict* rather than a *war*), we heard or read the phrase, "protective reaction strike," until we were numb and began to accept it as meaningful until suddenly its hypocrisy became apparent. Other examples of clichés (and illegitimate words) which have began to pall are *seize* (as in "seized of a problem") *viable, knowhow, frame of reference, rubric, dialogue, backstop, scenario, think pieces, phase out, bird-dog* (verb), "light at the end of the tunnel," *ambivalence,* "other side of the coin," and, of course, monstrosities like *surveil* and *liase,* which someone has called "a deformed, genetically uncivilized infinitive."

Most clichés are not gobbledygook in the sense that they obscure meanings. Many of them are once-bright metaphors, tarnished by overuse. Some are "in-words," admired and imitated ad nauseam: *clout, thrust, escalate, crunch, simplistic, boggle, visceral response, infrastructure,* and *orchestrate* are examples. Constantly repeated, they become irritants, detracting from clarity because the listener finds himself attending to the means of communication rather than to the message it is meant to convey. In everyday speech we get into the habit of using popular clichés without realizing that they may stand in the way of effective communication: *life-style, senior citizen, fun party,* "have a ball," "let's face it," "I have news for you," "get with it," "I've had it."

At the National War College several years ago, one of the students, Marine Colonel (now General) Ralph Spanjer, made a survey of the gobbledygook used by guest speakers at the College, all men of achievement. He concluded that there are four general varieties of contemporary triteness especially popular in governmental ("emphatically including military") and academic circles.

1. Some words, he decided, are simply trite: *boggle, time-frame, in-house.* 2. Others achieve triteness because of overuse: *thrust, credibility gap, scenario,* and *quantum jump.* 3. Some are foreign phrases excessively used: *vis-à-vis, quid pro quo, rapprochement, détente, caveat, a priori.* 4. Some are basically good, but atrociously overused: *ambivalent, expertise, dialogue, clout, spectrum.*

Fifty-one of the hundred speakers used the champion cliché *pragmatic* that year. Among the runners up were *vis-a-vis, dialogue, xenophobia, charisma, thrust, excerbate, dichotomy, hegemony, cost-effective, proliferation, counter-productive, quid pro quo, caveat, viable, ambivalence, scenario, escalate, expertise, low silhouette, quantum jump, flexible response, rapprochement, détente, simplistic, in-house, time frame, pluralistic, polycentrism,* and *infrastructure.*

An ingenious member of General Spanjer's class combined his list of gobbledygook words in a parody of Hamlet's famous soliloquy. Following are a few lines from that imaginative effort:

> To exacerbate or not to exacerbate, that is the dichotomy;
> Whether 'tis more viable vis-à-vis the mind to suffer
> The thrusts and boggles of outrageous escalation,
> Or to take arms against a sea or pragmatism,
> And by opposing, end them. To die, to crunch,
> No more, and by a crunch to say we end
> The xenophobia and the thousand counter-productive dialogues
> That flesh is heir to; 'tis an in-house ambivalence
> Devoutly to be opted, to die to sleep...

As long as we stand by unprotestingly and accept the assaults on our beautiful, flexible language, we deserve nothing better than the turgid, exasperating communication prevalent today. As long as newly fledged professionals admire and imitate the heinous jargon of their superiors, feeling that thereby they show their sophistication, gobbledygook will thrive. As long as those in high places produce verbal abortions like *persecutorial, confidentiality, prioritize, to auspice* and *to self-destruct,* which then become part of the national vocabulary, we'll have deterioration of the language. As long as those who object to "nebulous verbosity" and pretentious "bafflegab" are called enemies of usage, which is the justifier of any violation of grammar, pronunciation, and meaning the speaker or writer consciously or unconsciously makes, we are in danger of imprecise, ugly, and ineffective communication.

Let's stamp out gobbledygook!

GUILTY
of
language
hang-ups

Some Language Hang-Ups!

Most of us have language hang-ups: certain grammatical constructions or insecure words which we avoid, certain words which we overuse, idiosyncratic tricks of hesitation, grunting, interpolation of "y'know" or "I mean," illogical use of "like," gross mispronunciations, addiction to clichés, current slang, or jargon, and awkward sentence structure. Sometimes the hang-up is a general self-consciousness about speech. Because the speaker or writer is aware of his poverty-stricken vocabulary or his uncertainty about grammar, pronunciation, and idiom, he may be actively ashamed of his ignorance and reluctant to expose himself in conversation, letters, and official communications.

Examples of common hang-ups are the almost universal confusion over "who" and "whom" and "its" and "it's," which illustrate the inability of many American to master the objective and possessive cases; the addiction to pompous words or phrases like "prior to" for "before," "possess" for "have," "accomplish" for "do," and "reside" for "live," or fashionable gobbledygook like "parameter," "climate of opinion," "address the subject," "interface," cognizance," "infrastructure," failure to distinguish between "infer" and "imply," "principal" and "principle," "effect" and "affect."

Let's examine some of these difficulties and try to find remedies for them.

The who-whom syndrome

Those who have trouble with "who" and "whom" and with the five other words in English that still have objective forms should be grateful that

By Argus Tresidder, reprinted from the *Marine Corps Gazette* for February 1975.

they don't have to distinguish between the nominative and objective cases for all nouns. The language has been blessedly simplified so that nouns no longer have case endings which indicate whether they are subjects or objects. Six pronouns, however, still have objective cases: I, me; we, us; he, him; she, her; they, them; who, whom. When we use those words, we have to prove that we know the difference between a subject and an object. "Me and Joe had the duty." *No.* "This is between you and I." *No.* "Whom do you think would do a better job?" *No.* If a person says, "Thank you for the warm greeting you have extended to my wife and I," he is dead wrong about the "I." Such mistakes in the use of the objective case are the result of ignorance or carelessness.

"Who" and "whom," however, are often complicated by adjacent words and phrases and by the curious—and usually mistaken—idea that "whom" is more elegant than "who." For example, "Col. Avery, who many think will soon get his first star, is a fine officer." This sentence is quite correct because "who" is the subject of the verb "will get," not the object of the verb "think." In the question often asked by stylish secretaries, "Whom shall I say called?", "whom" should be "who," the subject of "called," not the object of "say." "Who did you introduce me to?" is wrong. "Whom do you want to see?" is correct. "Whom do you think will be elected?" is incorrect.

Remember "who" is the subject, "whom" the object. Don't let the words between the pronoun and the verb or preposition fool you. You probably wouldn't say, "For who the bell tolls," but you might easily say, "Who were you with last night?" (and some liberal grammarians tell us "who" is acceptable in sentences like this). "Who" is booby-trapped by phrases like "they say" and "some people think":

> **whom** (hōōm), *pron.* [ME. *whom, hwom;* AS. *hwam, aat.* of *hwa;* see WHO], the objective case of **who:** in colloquial usage, now often replaced by *who.*

► "The old man who many people think was crazy died in a fire." *Right:* "who...was crazy."
► "Whomever we finally select as captain must be passing in all his work." *Right:* "whomever is the object of "select". The whole phrase "whomever...captain" is the subject of "must be."
► "There was considerable doubt about whom should be elected." *Wrong:* "who" is the subject of "should be elected." The whole phrase is the object of the preposition "about."
► "I know it was he whom we had selected for the office." *Right:* "whom" is the object of "we had selected."

The "Y'know" habit

In the past, when a speaker groped for a word, he usually grunted "uh"; now he tends to say "y'know." The meaningless phrase becomes so addic-

94

tive that it often pushes its silly way into otherwise articulate speech. A recent cartoon showed a man in front of a TV set with a pad in his hand. "That's a new talk show record," he says. "136 'ya knows' in fifteen minutes." Another, in *The New Yorker,* showed a long-haired, gangling student reciting in an English class: "A rose is a...sort of like I mean a...you know...rose...is...like...you know...a rose...right?" Mark Lane, in his *Communications With Americans,* transcribes a verbatim interview with a soldier in Vietnam. It begins:

> I mean, you can't fight the Army, not one man. About this type of thing, you know. We were going out on day patrols with, you know, infantry cats that had been doing this a long time and they were teaching us several things. And then we had to pull night patrols—I mean the day patrols weren't bad—and then we had to pull night patrols and to pull guard on ammunition dumps and things like this. It was after a couple of months that, you know, things started getting hot like...

This kind of communication makes us sound like a society of morons, Yet there seems to be no cure for it except rigorous self-control like that of the person who gives up smoking. Among those who scorn controls, the wearers of slovenly clothes and messy hair, the school dropouts, the junkies, the generation-gap revolutionaries, sloppy speech habits might be expected. But "y'know," "I mean," and "like" seem to be as contagious as summer colds, and even disciplined speakers catch them.

Some experts think that "y'know" has to wear off like acne, leaving little scars on speech and even occasional late-blooming pustules. Others think it should be treated like a speech defect with drills and mechanical devices. I believe, however, that firm, friendly criticism, which should include "No, I don't know" whenever "y'know" proliferates and an occasional "For God's sake, say it without telling what *you* mean and what *I know,"* can do much to reduce the infection.

Gross mispronunciations and misspellings

It's a strange fact that many well-groomed people, who take pride in gleaming shoes and color harmony, are content with unpolished diction which shows them up just as relentlessly as excess fat, holes in their socks, and rude manners. I am constantly surprised to find that people trained to be keen observers, who would immediately spot a misplaced decimal point or a historical inaccuracy or a tactical error, are careless about the pronunciation of even common words and cheerfully admit that their spelling is wayward.

Why has the pronunciation *nuc-u-lar* become so widespread, though the correct spelling *nuclear* should be a clear guide? Notice how often *percolate* and *escalate* acquire a central $\bar{u}$ sound because the users have not paid atten-

---

ac·cu·ŗate (ak′yoo-rit), *adj.* [L. *accuratus,* pp. of *accurare*
< *ad-,* ţo′ + *curare,* to take care < *cura,* care], 1. careful
and exact. 2. free from mistakes or errors; precise.

95

tion to the correct vowel. Listen to the unwary wrap their tongues around *barbiturate, mischievous, irrevocable, accesory, chaise longue, formidable.* Dictionaries which permissively record usage, however faulty, rather than establish standards have failed to hold the line in words like *lamentable, irrefutable, harass, diphtheria, vehicle, precedence,* and *exquisite,* all now acceptable with "secondary" pronunciations unsanctioned thirty years ago.

Some mispronunciation is the result of ignorance or thoughtless imitation; much, however, is the fault of lazy lips, which produce slovenly diction, lazy eyes, which might note spellings or look up words, and lazy brains. Note how many put a *t* in the spoken *often* and an *h* at the end of *height,* say *accrit* for *accurate, rekanize* for *recognize, larnyx* for *larynx, orgy* with a hard *g, sinificant* for *significant, canidate* for *candidate,* and so on. Try the following five words on your friends. If they can correctly pronounce more than two of them they are extraordinarily observant: *coccyx, forte* (meaning the thing a person does especially well), *schism, flaccid, grimace. Unfortunately, schism* and *grimace* now have acceptable secondary pronunciations.

> **gri·mace** (gri-mās′). *n.* [Fr.; prob. adapted < OHG. *grimmiza* < base of *grim* (see GRIM)], a distortion of the face; a wry or ugly smile or facial expression of pain, contempt, etc., sometimes intended to amuse. *v.i.*

Flagrant misspellings, in the same way, are unnecessary confessions of ignorance. You may not have a good memory for English spelling, which is often chaotic, but your dictionary can help you not to show your weakness in public. Grind your teeth when you find you're still not sure about a word you've looked up many times, and look it up again, maybe nailing it down by association or some form of memory aid. Words like *occurred, sacrilegious, seize, perseverance, irrelevant, dependent, embarrass, weird, noticeable* bother most people. But spellings (and pronunciations) like *artic* for *arctic, similiar* for *similar, athalete* for *athlete, loose* for *lose, Febuary* for *February, ocassion* for *occasion, verbage* for *verbiage, minature* for *miniature, kimona* for *kimono,* are unforgivable.

Try the following five fiendish words on your friends. You'll be safe in betting that they won't be able to spell correctly more than one of them: *dessicate, vilify, rarefy, supersede, inoculate.*

The slippery pairs

Certain words which sound almost or exactly like other words create some hang-ups. Because they've never straightened out these pairs, people constantly and absurdly confuse them. The difference between *marital* and *martial,* for example, is only the position of the *i* and the *t,* but the difference in meaning, in spite of jokes, is enough to demand caution by the user. Other slippery pairs are *principal* and *principle, effect* and *affect, complement* and *compliment, appraise* and *apprise, emigrate* and *im-*

96

migrate, allusion and *illusion, imminent* and *eminent, incredible* and *incredulous, continual* and *continuous.*

A three-star general once told me that he must constantly be on the watch for the incorrect use of *appraise* and *apprise* in reports and letters drafted by senior officers for his signature. They cannot seem to understand that when you *appraise,* you set a value on or judge the quality of something; when you *apprise,* you inform or notify. You cannot *appraise* somebody of something; you *apprise* not *appraise* an estate or a rare stamp.

The difference between *principal* and *principle* is clear. Yet many people use one when they mean the other. When you want an adjective meaning first in rank or importance, it *must* be *principal. Principle* is always a noun, never an adjective *Principal* is both an adjective and a noun, but the noun means something quite different from *principle.* A *principal* is the head of a school or the main body of an estate as distinguished from income; a *principle* is a precept, a fundamental truth, or a rule of conduct. The *principal* (chief actor) in a play may be a man of no *principle* (ethical standards).

Effect and *affect* are so often confused that some users wince when they speak or write them, never sure which is which. The way to get them straight is to remember (1) that in normal usage only *effect* can be a noun, never *affect;* (2) that the verb *effect* means to bring about or accomplish (as "to effect a change"); (3) and that the verb *affect* means to influence (as "His stubbornness affected the outcome") or, in another sense, to pretend. When a person or thing influences or *affects* some one or something, he or it has an *effect* on that person or thing, but does not *effect* it. An easy formula: *Effect,* noun, impression, result, influence; or verb, to cause to happen; *affect,* verb, to influence.

Emigrate and *immigrate* are confusing only if you don't know that the *e* of emigrate means "from" and the *im-* of *immigrate* means "to." One *emigrates* from another country; he *immigrates* to a new country. At the point of departure he is *emigrating* and is called an *emigrant;* at the point of entry he is *immigrating* and is called an *immigrant.*

---

con·tin·u·al (kən-tin′ū-əl), *adj.* [ME. *continuele;* OFr. *continuel* < L. *continuus;* see CONTINUE]. 1. happening over and over again; repeated often; going on in rapid succession. 2. continuous; going on uninterruptedly.

An idea or a story is *incredible,* unbelievable; the person who doesn't believe is *incredulous.* Only a person can be *incredulous.* Something *imminent* is about to happen, impending. *Imminent* is miles away from *eminent,* which means outstanding, prominent. *Continual* and *continuous* have tended to merge in meaning, but those who make careful distinctions think of *continuous* as meaning without interruption (as "a continuous fall of snow"), of *continual* as recurring repeatedly ("continual discussions"). *Allusion* means reference; *illusion* means a false idea or perception. Confusion of *allusion* and *illusion* and *imminent* and *eminent* and *respectfully* and *respectively* is stupid. Other pairs, however, are closer in meaning and may puzzle even careful speakers.

One pair of unlike words is so frequently misused that a special effort must be made to get them right: *imply* and *infer.* A speaker or writer *implies;* a hearer or reader *infers.* The words are not interchangeable. A speaker never *infers to* an audience (though he may *infer from* what some one else has said). From what he implies or suggests, the audience *infers* a meaning not explicitly stated.

Addictive words

These are words and phrases which become stereotypes when too frequently and unvaryingly used. They have the same deadening effect on communication that *whereases* have on legal documents and *begats* on family trees. They reveal a lack of imagination and a supine conformity to convention in their chronic users that tend to make speech and writing colorless. For example, some people seem unable to speak of simple *time.* They must say "point in time" or "time-frame." *Problem* becomes "problem area." They never just *leave;* they *depart* (and incidentally and incorrectly make it into a transitive verb so that they "depart John's office" or "depart Seattle" instead of "depart from" or, better, *leave).* They don't *issue* order; they *promulgate* them. *Do* becomes *accomplish* (and because there's something noble about accomplishment the verb goes with *goal, mission, problem, achievement,* and other incongruous objects). Everything, from health to character, is *outstanding. After* is too simple a word; it must be *subsequent to.* Nothing ever *happens;* it *transpires.* A word addict can't say he *lives* in a certain town; he *resides* there. He doesn't *own* a house; he *possesses* it.

Two currently addictive words are *hopefully* and *additionally,* both nearly always grammatically incorrect as synonyms for "I (we) hope" and "moreover" or "in addition." So is the phrase "address a question" or, worse, "address an area." Others are *clout, escalate, environment, orchestrate, scenario, spectrum, posture, optimize, -wise* (as in *time-wise), input, in-house.*

Many addictive words are, of course, the cliché of the moment, which will be replaced by others as fashions change. For example, the tiresome phrase, "climate of opinion" has already begun to fade, and nonce words like *natch, fantabulous,* and *pazazz* have almost disappeared. Two of the most irritating at the present time are "tell it like it is" and "doing your own thing." *Schlock* and *schtick* are now among the sophisticated clichés. Others are borrowed from *hip* talk, and those who like to be admired for their quick adjustment to tie-width, long sideburns, and "in" opinions speak glibly of *rapping* or being *uptight* or *spaced-out.* In such conformist speech people *dig* rather than understand, *cop-out* rather than take the easy way, and *rip-off* instead of steal Sometimes the addicts are cute, full of precious expressions like *anyhoo, all rightie,* and *togetherness.* They like to make up new combinations, using current suffixes like *-wise, -nik,* and *-ize:*

98

computer-wise, dogood-nik, nudenik, peacenik, definitize, maximize, containerize, randomize, suboptimize.

Much of the gobbledygook which forms malignant cysts on professional communication today is as contagious as words like *hopefully* are addictive. Some one develops the first lesion, inventing a new word, distorting the meaning of an old one, or overemphasizing a technical or abstract term. His associates, if they envy his learning enough to imitate him or if they think the addition to the vocabulary of their discipline is impressive and will be understood only by the initiate (or if they don't understand but like the sound of the word or don't want anybody to know they don't understand) are easily infected. They spread the disease.

Take for example the word *interface*. The Department of Defense *Dictionary* defines it fuzzily as "a boundary or point common to two or more similar or dissimilar command and control systems, sub-systems, or other entities against which or at which necessary information flow takes place." This is an extension of the basic meaning of the word: "a surface that lies between two parts of matter or space and forms their common boundary." It sounds so impressive that *interface* has been enthusiastically taken up by gobbbledygook specialists everywhere, who for the most part haven't the slightest idea what it really means. They have arbitrarily turned it into a verb (though its only acceptable use is as a noun), which is an insupportable synonym for *confront*. So popular has this piece of gobbledygook become that *The New Yorker* recently printed a cartoon showing two Madison Avenue or State Department types. One says to the other, "As a favor to an old pal, Ted, what the hell *does* 'interface' mean?"

---

in·ter·face (in′tĕr-fãs′). *n.* a surface that lies between two parts of matter or space and forms their common boundary.

Parameter is another example of word abuse. It is a mathematical term meaning "a quantity or constant whose value varies with the circumstances of its application, as the radius line of a group of concentric circles, which varies with the circle under consideration." At first it no doubt had this precise technical meaning. But it had too impressive a sound and the touch of vagueness necessary to true gobbledygook to be allowed to remain in mathematical obscurity. Those who tossed it off knew that most hearers had no idea what it meant but envied the users their *savoir faire*. The word became almost a status symbol until imitators ruined it by distorting its meaning. Now for many it's just a fancy word for *perimeter*, pretentiously and ridiculously overused.

Technical words are not in themselves gobbledygook, and no one should object when aviators or computer specialists or diplomats or teachers of education speak to each other in thick globules of language. Those who believe that the most essential element of communication is clarity may doubt that even the experts really know what they are talking about and suspect that they are using their esoteric vocabulary simply to impress their colleagues or to demonstrate to the outside world how profound their subject is. Nevertheless, within their own group they have inalienable rights. If they expect to be understood outside that group, however, they should be willing to translate their overloaded, usually Latin- or Greek-based words into plain English. When they do not, they lay themselves open to the suspicion that they *don't* know what they are talking about. Or it may be—or that, because what they have to say is too unimportant or too illogical to be exposed to the merciless light of clarity or because for reasons of "security" or diplomatic or professional expediency they prefer to be imprecise, their communication is fog-bound.

> **per·im·e·ter** (pə-rim′ə-tĕr), *n.* [L. *perimetros; Gr. peri-metros* < *peri-*, around + *metron*, a measure], **1.** the outer boundary of a figure or area: as, a fence marked the *perimeter* of the field. **2.** the total length of this. **3.**

Let's look at a few examples. No one these days is fired or discharged; he is *disestablished, reduced-in-force, terminated, involuntarily retired, defunded,* or *de-staffed.* Business men seem to like resonant phrases like "in the normal course of our procedure" rather than "normally," "of the order of magnitude of" instead of "about" or "approximately," "pursuant to our agreement" instead of "as we agreed," and "supervisory verification" for "approval." The newly elite computer specialists have established their claim to respect by inventing a vocabulary of jargon which includes obese phrases like "maximum system integration," "automatic flowcharting and environmental monitorizing," "trip hierarchy modeling," "computerized flow simulations," "data-oriented network restructurings." Art critics, perhaps concealing their bewilderment, come up with comments on contemporary artists such as "There is a singular combining of the purely somatic and the archly conceptualized and verbal in his aesthetic cognition." Even the U.S. Postal Service has its special "in-house" gobbledygook, of which the following is a sample:

> The data will be of value in increasing the depth-of-fact and reducing the price handling by enabling the regional staffs to optimize their sweepside diagrams.

Education enters the lists with what is perhaps the most turgid phraseology of all; e.g., "Major categories in the cognitive domain of the taxonomy of educational objectives." The Department of Defense comes up with such masterly inflation of meaning as "The magnitude of the problem is not easily susceptible to quantification."

There is no easy cure for gobbledygook. It is epidemic in our society. Scholars and technicians and bureaucrats lose face if they do not reveal a jaunty familiarity with the jargon of their trade. The result is that since some of them are ashamed to admit that they're not entirely sure what the buzz-words mean, the words get lost in the fog-banks of poor communication. I suggest two means of combating gobbledygook:

1. self-discipline, which demands the deliberate building up of mental lists of words you will not, under any circumstances, use;

2. deflation, which involves questioning of all who speak in gobbledygook, "Now what the hell does that mean?"

I have so far discussed the most common language hang-ups which detract from effective communication. My final hang-up is less definite than the others. It is the acute self-consciousness of those who are so uncertain of their grammar, pronunciation, and idiom that they stand in their own light. They may fail to make the most of excellent talents because they know that what they write or say will make them seem semi-illiterate. It may indeed. The senior officer or company official or civil servant who is unable to organize his ideas logically and to express them clearly is not likely to get rapid promotion because ability to communicate is increasingly important in executives, administrators, and professional leaders of all kinds. There is decreasing hope of promotion for the man or woman who failed dum-dum English in college or who has a chronic case of "y'knows," faulty pronunciations, and limited vocabulary when he gets up to speak.

What can be done about an otherwise able person who has trouble expressing himself? For one thing, he can do some strenuous restudy of English, either in adult education or community college courses or in programmed self-study, such as Joseph C. Blumenthal's *English 3200* (Harcourt, Brace, and World, 1972). He can join a Toastmasters' group, take a speed-reading course, get a good dictionary, seek informed comment on his writing, and become an observant and critical reader and listener.

He might begin by analyzing his particular language hang-ups and becoming aware of them in others.

In Defense Of Language Standards

The trend of the times is to reduce language to unattractive jargon, disregard basic rules of grammar, idiom, and pronunciation, and stupidly or ignorantly accept the slovenly belief that there is no standard except usage. If enough people make the same mistakes, distort meanings of the same words, repeat the same gibberish, copy the same mispronunciations, the believers in this doctrine think, they make their new usage acceptable. The result is a falling off in effective communication, an invasion of linguistic barbarisms, and a weakening of the most beautiful, flexible, and widely used language in the world.

The transcripts of White House conversations during the Watergate period give us some bleak examples of the low level to which communication has sunk. They reveal the lack of clear thinking, the impoverished vocabularies, the awkward syntax of those who participated, typical of much speaking and writing in our time. Here are a few random samples:

> "That's good, because I find—incidentally, if I might—I don't think I like—for example, I haven't been in touch with John Mitchell but he might call me sometime and I don't want to be in a position of ever saying, anything, see?"
>
> "The hang-out road's going to have to be rejected." "I, some, I understand it was rejected."

By Argus Tresidder reprinted from the *Marine Corps Gazette* for April, 1976.

"Third Floor: londjeray and chase lounges."

"That's why your, for your immediate thing you've got no choice with
Hunt but the hundred and twenty or whatever it is." Right?
John Dean...concludes, concurs now with Mitchell's recommendation that
the only way to solve this, and we're set up beautifully to do it, also is that...That
the way to handle this now is for us to have Walters call Pat Gray and just say
"Stay to hell out of this—this is, ah, business here we don't want you to go any
further on it." That's not an unusual development, and ah, that would take care
of it.

Careless speakers and their allies, the structural linguists who have only
passing respect for the historical development of individual words and scorn
the idea of language standards, are trying to democratize English. They
believe that a head count of current usage, no matter how much that usage
is based on error, confusion with other words, lack of knowledge of
etymology, or just plain carelessness, is more important than past standards. They are in general undiscriminating about whose heads they count.
If buyers and sellers of cheap furniture talk about bedroom *suits,* that's fine
with them. Because most Americans are unfamiliar with French (or Latin or
German or any other language than their own), they don't know any better
than to make the French *chaise longue* into a *chaise* (pronounced "chase")
lounge; the elevator operator's "Third Floor, londjeray" becomes
established as the *preferred* pronounciation in the Third edition of the Merriam Webster New International Dictionary (which I shall call Merriam III);
clique may be "click" and *chic* "chick"; *buffet, cabaret* and *ballet,* like
valet, have acquired final t sounds; *bona fide* becomes "bonnafide" and
vice versa "vais-versa." What used to be regarded as nonce words, popular
slang bound to disappear, are now solemnly included by Merriam without
label or comment that would identify them for what they are. Among them
are *barf,* an unnecessary synonym for "vomit," *bonkers,* "crazy," *Mickey
Mouse* as an adjective meaning "insignificant," *gangbang, freebie,* and *go-
go.* Others are *nudie, kook, deli* (short for delicatessen), *boo* (marijuana),
pizzazz, zonked, zap, kinky, limo (short for limousine), *boffo, bummer,
dinch, hipness, ricky tick.*
More terrifying in their influence on language pollution than the appearance of foolish or unnecessary words and changes brought about by
usage is the increase in words with impressive sound but vague meaning,
barbarisms, monstrosities, and deliberately faulty grammar. Speakers and
writers who do not want to be held responsible for exact meanings, or who
hope to conceal ignorance, hunt for big, Latinized, abstract words that
make them seem to know more than they do or else are comfortably ambiguous.

Sometimes the communicators are simply too lazy to check what they
assume is correct—or at least common—usage and continue to abuse good
words like *rhetoric, disinterested,* and *infer,* all of which have lost their true

meanings, at least in some slovenly vocabularies. *Disinterested* has now been used so often to mean "uninterested" that we must now explain when

---

"He went bonkers after one drag on the boo."

---

we mean it in its primary—and once unique—sense of "impartial." Politicians and media writers have almost completely changed the meaning of *rhetoric,* which *should* mean "the art or science of using words effectively in speaking and writing," to refer to high-flown, misleading, or lying oratory. *Infer* may now be used as meaning exactly the same as *imply.* Three good words have gone down the drain of inexact use. Their primary meanings have almost been lost.

Two words, one made familiar by Watergate, the other by Presidents who appropriated it to their special use so that now it has only their arbitrary meaning, are *stonewall* and *jawbone,* both respectable nouns that have been made into rather silly verbs. *Stonewall,* once a property marker or barrier or the sobriquet of a Civil War hero, now suggests a stubborn unwillingness to tell the truth. As a verb it surprisingly comes from a British cricket term meaning to bat defensively. The British also use it to refer to debate or other parliamentary tactics for the purpose of consuming time and thus obstructing procedure or business. Mr. Nixon has added a meaning which will no doubt appear in the Fourth Edition of the Merriam Webster. *Jawbone* just made it among the addenda in the Third Edition as *jawboning,* "a strong appeal by a chief of state to national business and labor leaders for price and wage restraints." Among the main entries

---

"Avoid immersing me in a state of dysphoria."

---

jawbone is a noun with only a slang meaning in addition to its basic meaning of "mandible": "credit, trust, as to get supplies on *jawbone.*" Presidents Johnson and Nixon both used it as a verb with the meaning of using the jaws (a synecdoche for the mechanism of speech) to keep down prices and wages. It's a far cry from the weapon with which Samson slew the Philistines.

This tendency for words to acquire secondary meanings quite different from their primary meanings, either because they *sound* like or *suggest* other words or because users are ignorant or careless, comes under what a contemporary guardian of good English, Theodore Bernstein, calls "Bernstein's Second Law." In his book *The Careful Writer* (1973) he defines his Second Law as holding that

> Bad words tend to drive out good ones, and when they do, the good ones never appreciate in value, sometimes maintain their value, but most often lose in value, whereas the bad words may remain bad or get better.

He gives as examples of such words *enormity,* misused for *enormousness; transpire,* misused for *happen;* and *glamour,* which primarily means deceptive charm or enchantment, but which now means anything from beauty to style. *Noisome,* of course, has nothing to do with noise, any more than *fatuous* describes corpulence, or *fulsome* means full. Bernstein is especially irritated by the use of powerful words such as *awful, dreadful, fearful,* or *horrible* which are used in "commonplace expressions of disapproval (or approval)." His list of these words, which he calls "atomic flyswatters," includes *adorable, colossal, divine, fabulous, fantastic, frightful, sensational,* and *terrific.*

The monstrosities are ugly words that have crept out of swamps into the language, like Beowuulf's Grendel. Many of them have -ize and -wise endings: *prioritize, optimize, conceptualize, definitize, civilianize,* P.R.*-wise, logisticalwise.* Others are absurd back-formations like *orientate* and *commentate* or bastardized verbs from nouns like *liaise* from *liaison, surveil* from *surveillance, attrit* from *attrition.* Many monstrous words are the product of restless tendency to make nouns into verbs: *to structure, to input, to interface, to suspicion, to decision, to destruct.* But we are also good at turning other parts of speech into Mongoloids: *commonality, bodifier, chairperson, biztalk, meritocracy, opinionating, micromobility, ghettonomics, disincentive, somatopsychic.* English is in danger of being taken over by trolls, lugging their misbegotten creations out of dank fens.

Though much language pollution is the fault of excessively technical, illegitimate, muddy, or overused *words,* much more comes from *phrases* and *sentences* that do violence to English grammar or conceal meanings, either

---

"The ambiguous nuances of the vertical analysis."

---

because the writer or speaker doesn't know any better or does not want to be held accountable for what he says. Often these cloudy or ambiguous phrases are built from words which by themselves make sense, but which together produce gobbledygook: "historical eclecticism," "protective reaction," "democratic centralism," "economic determinism," "preemptive strike," "widely affirmative trends," "frame of reference," "cultural empathy," "ideological freight," "prepositional guide lines," "ceiling in slots," "rubric of this area," "systematized monitored capability," "time frame," "maximum system integration," "running out of the bottom line," and so on endlessly. Usually, however, they are intended to impress, whether or not they convey meaning, and are made up of jargonized words: "ambiguous nuances of the actual," "historicist doctrines," "withdrawal-affiliated sortie," "vertical analysis," "judgmental evaluation," "cognitive domain," "interest inventory," "technical interface concepts." Such phrases blossom into sentences which anger, puzzle, or put to sleep the reader or hearer, like the following:

> Kindly effectuate a termination. Avoid immersing me in a state of dysphoria.
> Families who cling to ethnic traditions may encourage a participatory orientation toward death by their reliance upon patterns of personal interaction rather than institutionalized procedures.

The interdisciplinary or supportive input will encapsulate vertical team structure.

Failure to properly return executed forms prior to the specified date will result in entitlement to increase in quarters allowance for dependents receiving negative substantiation on official pay records which will be discontinued.

Bennett Cerf once kidded the makers of such pompous, ostentatious phrases by turning the advice: "Be intelligible, think for yourself, and be brief," into

> Beware of platitudinous ponderosity. Let your communication process possess coalescent consistency and concatenated cogency. Eschew all flatulent garrulity and asinine affectations. Use intelligibility and veracious vivacity without rodomontade or thrasonical bombosity. Sedulously avoid all prolixity and psittaceous vacuity.

Finally, we come to the polluters who abuse basic grammar and, by adding to the structural linguists' head-count, make error and ignorance acceptable. For example, an Army noncommissioned officer assigned to the preparation of a phrase- and word-book for his French peers sent for training to the United States, translated one sentence as "He laid on the bed." When some one pointed out that *laid* should have been *lay,* he defended his version by declaring that *laid* is what 90 per cent of GIs say, and his instruction was to supply average Americanisms. "Tell it like it is," "where it's at," "you ain't seen nothin' yet," "between you and I," "those sort of people," "these kind of magazines," "this type player," "I gotta do somethin' about them tapes," "me and Joe gonna be on duty tonight" have

---

"Sedulously avoid all...psittaceous vacuity."

---

become so commonplace that some uncivilized Americans feel that they are being pretentious if they say these things in any other way.

"For free," now recorded in Merriam III as a synonym for *gratis,* was originally a heavily humorous substitute for "for nothing." There is no need whatsoever for "for," but the bad joke continues and is accepted as standard. "Gonna" and "gotta" have not yet made it in Merriam, but rock singers, who know no other spellings of "going to" and "got to" (who ever says "must"?), and everday usage by other careless speakers have made them normal. The absurd "aren't I," used coyly by those who wouldn't be caught dead saying "ain't I," is sanctioned by Merriam. "He don't" and "we was," like "ain't," seem to be faltering under the attacks of elementary school teachers, but the six pronouns which still have objective cases, especially *whom,* still baffle many people. Even the grammarians have begun to weaken and accept *who* for *whom* in sentences like "Who were you with last night?" Most of us now accept "it's me" as an easy way out in colloquial speech, and "it's us," "it's her," and "it's them" will probably soon get official approval. Since most people have only a faint recollection of the rule that a preposition governs nouns in the objective case, usage has begun to erode the few objective forms we have left in the language: "A farewell dinner is planned for he and his wife on Friday," "Thank you for

---

"Every woman should have their choice."

---

the warm greeting you have extended to Mrs. Nixon and I," "Between you and he there's some bad feeling."

The difference between *affect* and *effect, principle* and *principal, lie* and *lay, sit* and *set, infer* and *imply, flaunt* and *flout, appraise* and *apprise, between* and *among,* because writers and speakers are too damned lazy to learn it, has already become vague. Careless or ignorant use of number in agreement between nouns and verbs and pronouns and their antecedents has produced a generation which blandly accepts "Every woman should have their choice," "Fred Jones, along with hundreds of other farmers, are forced to start all over again," "Music written by Beethoven, Haydn, and Mozart have been neglected in America."

When headlines in major newspapers announce that "Data Reveals Secrets" and "The Media Is in Trouble," we can't hope that *memoranda, curricula, criteria, strata,* and *phenomena* will remain plurals. We've already accepted *agenda* as a singular. Since few of us study Latin nowadays, I suppose we should not be surprised that Latin words taken over bodily into English are abused. The confused pronunciation of foreign words has made us uncertain whether *alumni* and *alumnae* are males or females, and words and phrases like *via, re, non compos mentis, nouveau riche, hors d' oeuvres, milieu, genre, sine qua non, sang froid, vertebrae, antennae, formulae, de jure, per se, consortium, corpus delecti, lèse majesté, subpoena, apotheosis, habeas corpus* become almost unrecognizable. The effort to give Latin and Greek words ending in -is their proper plurals is a curious kind of word snobbery which often goes astray: the plural of *basis* is *bases,* pronounced with two long vowels; the plural of

---

"Like it's real, man, to do your own thing."

---

base also spelled *bases,* has only one long vowel. The snobs mix them up, as they do the plural of *crisis,* which at least one speaker showing off his learning turned into *criseses.*

Let's pull the curtain over such current horrors as "like it's real, man," "do your own thing," "it isn't all that important," "Springfield Mall is something else," "it's like cold," "he's some kind of a nut," "them kind," "hadn't ought to do it," "drug" (past tense of *drag),* "slud" (past tense of *slide).*

Why have we allowed this deterioration of our ability to communicate? It is not from lack of examples of eloquence. Within our time we've listened to lovers of words like Winston Churchill, Adlai Stevenson, John Kennedy,

Robert Frost, Ernest Hemingway, and Maxwell Anderson, who could have been our examples rather than the ghost-writers of most politicans, the writers of bureaucratic reports, the novelists like Norman Mailer and Kurt Vonnegut, the purveyors of gobbledygook on television who spread the hideous habits of our generation. In a period of generally lowered standards—of behavior, manners, morals, workmanship, art, education, and so on—it is not surprising that we have a corresponding falling off in our standards of oral and written communication.

Let's be fair, however. Usage has been and will continue to be a powerful influence on language. In the long run it determines the course and effects the changes by which language grows. If over a period of time long enough to eliminate the ephemeral words and the transient errors, new words and idioms and pronunciations and, perhaps, spellings stay in the usage of opinion-formers, they *must* become standard. The word *rationale,* somewhere between 1934 and 1961, lost a syllable and the fancy pronunciation of "RAY-shun-AY-lee" and became a sensible "RASH-un-al." The recessive accent that now puts the emphasis on the first syllable in words like *research, address, adult, abdomen, cigarette, magazine* has almost wiped out the old pronunciations. What began as simple error in the pronunciation of *route* as *rout* has become ineradicable. The Greek sound of f in the letter *phi,* used in words like *diphtheria, diphthong,* and *amphitheatre* has all but disappeared. Those old standbys of the pedant, *congeries* and *vagary,* have lost their former tricky pronunciations. *Schism* and *flaccid* are about to join them. New, useful words like *astronaut, drip-dry, panty-hose, teen-ager, radar, nylon, backlog, deadline, bottleneck,* must appear, as times and manners change. Among the 100,000 new words recorded by Merriam III that developed in English between the 2nd and 3rd editions 17,000 were in the field of chemistry alone. No doubt the advances in science require those new words. Thank God most of us don't have to know them, but they are very welcome as legitimate additions to English. Not many of these contribute to the pollution. They prove that English is a vital, growing language.

Let's also be fair about the flexibility of American English, which permits more than one pronunciation of many words, many dialectal variations in idiom, pronunciation, and vocabulary, wide differences between formal

---

"me and Joe gonna be on duty tonight."

---

and informal, academic and colloquial, even young and old speech. We have several acceptable regional dialects (whose differences, unfortunately, are diminishing because of the leveling influence of radio and television). Moreover, the American characteristic of independence rejects pontification by experts or would-be experts in matters of language, as well as dress, customs, religion, and politics.

We have no national Commission, as some countries do, notably France, to protect the purity of the language and issue caveats about what new words or idioms are or are not acceptable. Neither do we have a national theatre or unofficial body of academic specialists to set standards of spelling, pronunciation, idiom, and meaning. No one region of the United States is regarded as having diction superior to that of other regions, as in England. Our radio and television networks, though they tend to homogenize usage, are not given the respect accorded the BBC by the British so that their speakers set general standards. We don't even have one dictionary to which we can turn for resolution of linguistic problems, as the British turn to the Oxford English Dictionary. We used to have the Webster *New International,* which set standards for pronunciation and usage, but since its editors, in the Third Edition, decided that language is democratic and that what some? many? anybody? says is worth recording, we only have a fat wordbook.

The American Heritage Dictionary, in a small way, has tried to settle some questions of usage by submitting controversial phrases, grammatical structure, pronunciation, and taste to a panel of specialists, recording their opinions in percentages for or against. There is some merit in this scheme, which at least doesn't accept the "scholarly" decision of the Merriam editors that anything goes, but the *American Heritage Dictionary* is not comprehensive enough, and its panel is too small and too eclectic to be authoritative. Still, the effort is in the right direction: that general usage in itself is not a sound criterion since it gives too much scope to ignorance and error, but that the judgments of educated, traveled, intelligent people, within their own dialectal areas, about what is provincial, vulgar, colloquial, wrong, should at least be available.

Many of the words I've mentioned as having changed in meaning and pronunciation or having been invented by hippies or junkies or computer specialists or sociologists may be justified on the basis of need, since we lack words for new developments in science, agriculture, industry, etc., or legitimate, long-term usage. They are in fact only minor threats to the language. When Mr. Nixon declared that he was "not going to cop out, but to hack it and tough it out," he was not contributing to verbal elegance, but he must have felt his use of current slang phrases made him seem to be an "in-person" rather than a remote, austere schemer. Colloquial speech has a sort of verve, before it begins to fade (unless it is marred, as in the following sentences, by intensive "y' knows" and "I means" and the atrocious misuse of "like")" "Y'know, like it's really groovy...I mean they really dig each other, y'know. Like well, they're not uptight, y'know. I mean like they really enjoy their thing." We can be somewhat tolerant of this kind of terrible communication because we know it is ephemeral and we can always hope that the next fashion in the speech of youth will be more attractive.

I have tried to describe the permissive, faulty, ambiguous usage of today that pollutes the once clear stream of the English language, turning it into a kind of murky, open-sewer river. Those who believe that growth comes only through change and that the "living" language is what the many make it, no matter how wrong they are or how little they know of etymology or of

109

basic grammar or how unaccustomed they are to clear thinking, can no doubt point to past threats to the purity of English, which it has survived. Changes came more slowly then, and the media were less powerful and less omnipresent. The Saxon base could easily absorb the influence of Latin and the flood of Norman words that changed the whole character of English. A hundred years passed between the first and second editions of the Webster New International Dictionary, but only twenty-seven years before the Third Edition was considered necessary. We'll soon need a Fourth Edition to register all the nonsense and evil inventions and loose changes in meaning and pronunciation that have been "sanctioned" since 1961.

Fortunately, voices continue to cry out in the wilderness of modern communication. It is comforting to learn that backers of English, who have been almost overwhelmed by the onslaughts of gobbledygook artists carrying banners labeled "Pedagogy," "Statecraft," "Computer Science," "Social Studies," "Management," and "Pentagon" rather than "Excelsior," have begun to rally. Their subject has become almost as obsolete in schools and colleges as Latin and Logic, partly through their own fault, since they have been more interested in discovering obscure 19th century poets or counting the use of litotes and meiosis in Milton than in teaching the effective use of the language. Some of them now look beyond eradication of *ain't,* split infinitives, and prepositions at the end of sentences and are taking alarm at what is happening to our great, flexible international medium of communication. Some of them have recently organized a Committee on Public Doublespeak to combat the influence on English of advertisers, politicians, and TV commentators. They even venture to suggest that they should emphasize detection of guile, deception, lack of clarity, and vague reasoning as much as grammar. More power to them! Let's get back to some standards!

110